Clarissa's Comfort Food

CLARISSA DICKSON WRIGHT

Clarissa's Comfort Food

Photography by Lisa Linder

Kyle Cathie Limited

To Sonic – always comforting and ready to eat the mistakes

Introduction

The idea for this book came about when I was touring for my autobiography, 'Spilling the Beans'. At each and every question-and-answer session following my talks, the same question came up: what would I cook when I got home? And because, by the end of the tour, I had been away from home for three and a half months, the answers to this question became something I fantasised about. This should have been the easiest of books to write, and while preparing the recipe list over the Christmas holidays, I looked forward to the project with enthusiasm. The saying, 'If you want to make God laugh, tell him your plans,' comes to mind, however, as for me this has turned out to be the hardest book I have ever written.

On 14 January I was driven out of my home by dry rot. I should have been back within two weeks, but due to the incompetence and dilatoriness of the builders, I remained cast out of my home and my kitchen. Writing a book on my favourite comfort foods whilst visiting other people's houses and kitchens is, I think, ironic. The Cholmondley Arms in Cheshire and the Goring Hotel in London helped to preserve my sanity, and my friend Sally allowed me the run of her kitchen. Indeed, this book is dedicated to her old greyhound Holyground Girl, winner of the Anglia Cup (the only 64-dog coursing stake besides the Waterloo Cup). Sonic, as she is known, had an endless appetite for disposing of any mistakes and was a constant comfort to me as I worked. Added to all this, the hard drive on my laptop crashed and there were endless sending problems with the replacement and its external modem.

But finally it was done, and I do hope you like it. Please bear in mind that this is my comfort food; if there are dishes you think should be included then you will have to write them into the back of the book yourself! I have spent a lifetime with food, and at sixty my tastes are fairly established. You will notice an absence of mushrooms because, sadly, I became allergic to them three years ago and can't even handle them, let alone eat them. The lack of carrots is simply because I dislike them intensely. (If you want to know why, read 'Spilling the Beans'.)

Growing up in my family, food was the only unifying factor. My father was a gourmet of considerable seriousness, and the food produced by our cook Louise, who had trained at Chatsworth and worked hand in glove with my mother, was always of the best standard. On weekdays, I was allowed to choose what I wanted to eat at lunchtime (within reason of course), provided that I ate what was put in front of me in the evening. This meant that I ate a more varied array of dishes and ingredients than your average child. Moreover we travelled a great deal – I had circled the globe three times by the time I was thirteen. We stayed in luxury hotels, but ate at roadside shacks and local restaurants as well. It was in Brazil at the age of four that I first realised that people in different countries ate different foods, and fejouda remains one of my favourites. Also, with my mother being born in Penang and my grandmother having lived in Singapore, Chinese and Malaysian dishes were a strong influence, too. I have spent time in the West Indies and love their dishes, and, of course, Europe had not yet been Americanised in my youth. Recently, I was in Brussels and found that the little restaurant I used to go to in the Galleries St Hubery, with my grandmother and my Belgian Aunt Emmy, was still there and still serving the best eel in green sauce. The waiters were just as rude and the service just as slow, but the food was just as good.

Have fun making your own lists of favourite recipes and tell me about them when we meet on my travels. I was on the road for some 100 days before I got to go home and write this book, so don't ever resent your own kitchen – just enjoy it for its comfort and familiarity.

Breakfast

'Breakfast like a king' is an old adage that is dear to my heart. When I was growing up we were always required to be down for breakfast at 8 a.m., no matter if the night before had been late and riotous or even if I went back to bed afterwards. It is a discipline that has stood me in good stead: on those occasions when I am at home and long to stay in bed, I seldom do so once thoughts of breakfast – one of my favourite meals – beckon.

After a lifetime of Hunt Balls, late-night parties and drink, my breakfast choices can often be eccentric: cold curry (once a feature of Hunt Balls) is still a pleasure, lard seasoned with paprika and spread on toast (recalling visits to southern Spain), or devilled pheasant legs (a throwback to shooting breakfasts). For now, however, I shall keep my frivols to myself and tell you about some of the more widely acceptable of my comfort breakfasts.

Porridge

First and foremost is porridge. With Scottish ancestry and living, as I do, in the country, I know that porridge must be made with water and a pinch of salt. When a notable food writer once suggested to my friend Isabel that porridge could be made with milk, she replied that people called that puppy sick, and promptly stopped him in his tracks. There is a splendid porridge stall at the Edinburgh Farmers' Market, offering the dish with many and various flavours from whisky to marmalade to cinnamon. But I still eat mine with salt.

When my grandfather worked as a doctor in the slums of Glasgow, the tenement dwellers would make a batch of porridge once a week and pour it into a lined drawer. They would then cut off a slice as required and either eat it cold or reconstitute it in boiling water. People shudder at the thought, but I am reminded of polenta when I think of this.

There are different grades of oats, some which can be made up on the spot and some which need overnight soaking. Pinhead oatmeal is the most textured and, to my mind, the most delicious type; however, it does need to be soaked overnight, unless you have an AGA, in which case it can be cooked overnight in the slow oven and finished on the top in the morning. Medium-ground oatmeal is the most commonly used, whilst finely ground oatmeal makes an invalid-style gruel rather than porridge, and is best kept for oatcakes, baking or other cooking, such as coating herrings.

Those of us who have survived the perils of boarding-school food will know only too well the horrors of burnt porridge. It takes only a momentary lapse of concentration for the oats to catch, so I always cook mine in a double boiler, preferably an enamel one. That wonderful Scottish implement the spurtle is the best thing for stirring porridge and breaking up any lumps, especially if you are reheating it.

I put two handfuls of pinhead oatmeal (for two portions) into the top of a double boiler with a pinch of salt and enough water to cover it well, then leave it to soak overnight. In the morning, I stir it well, put the pan into its base full of boiling water and leave it to simmer, stirring from time to time, for about 20–30 minutes. I then eat it with cold milk and, I am afraid to admit, a dusting of sugar.

It makes enough for two days, so I reheat the rest the following day by pouring boiling water on it, stirring well and simmering in the double boiler again for about 10–15 minutes.

There is an enzyme in heated oats which cuts cholesterol and is, indeed, the basis of the products, margarines and such likes that make the boast, how much nicer to eat porridge oats. If you must just make instant porridge but it is still better for you than commercial nostrums.

Kippers

It is hard to get good kippers nowadays – not for want of smokers, but for want of herrings. Stocks are depleted and the fish are much smaller than they used to be. Herrings were first kippered in 1861 at Craister in Northumberland and it was recorded, 'Today we smoked herrings as salmon is smoked in Scotland'. When we were filming for 'Two Fat Ladies' at a smokery in Whitby, which produced delicious kippers, we discovered that there are 79 words in the Lord's Prayer and, at that time, 3875 words in the Brussels governances on kippers! Last year I was on the Isle of Man, and the food was filthy in my hotel, but even they couldn't ruin the kippers. My own fishmonger Davy Clarke of Fisher Row, Musselburgh, smokes a very good kipper, but then you might expect this, as the town was once a port on the herring road.

The trick with kippers is to cook them in such a way that the whole house doesn't reek. I put mine, tails up, in a jug of very, very hot water (not quite boiling) and leave them to stand for 5–10 minutes, depending on size. I then flash them under the grill with a knob of butter (but this last is not strictly necessary).

Alternatively, a friend of mine poaches them in equal parts of milk and water with a little butter for about 6 minutes.

Kipper and caper pie

Whilst we are on the subject of kippers, try this rather strange little pie – against all one's preconceptions it is yummy.

SERVES 4

55g butter
55g flour
600ml milk
salt and pepper

450g kipper fillets, cooked
1½ tablespoons capers
450g puff pastry
1 hard-boiled egg, sliced
1 egg, beaten

Make a roux with the flour and butter and add the milk slowly to make a white sauce. Season, remove from the heat and add the kippers and the capers. Leave to cool.

Roll out the pastry into a 20cm square. Place the cooled kipper mixture in the centre, layered with the slices of hard-boiled egg. Brush the edges of the pastry with beaten egg and fold the corners in to make an envelope shape. Pinch the edges together, seal with more beaten egg, then brush the whole pie with the remaining egg. Bake for about 30 minutes or until golden.

Devilled Kidneys

More of a brunch or a supper dish since I stopped drinking, but good for a shooting breakfast; the Victorians loved devilled dishes for breakfast. The devilled butter can be used with pheasant or partridge, chicken or what you will, as well as with kidneys.

SERVES 4

2 shallots, finely minced
8 lamb kidneys, skinned, halved, cores removed

FOR THE DEVILLED BUTTER
225g butter

1½ tablespoons dried mustard
2 teaspoons Worcestershire sauce
2 teaspoons anchovy essence or Harvey's sauce or mustard ketchup
salt and cayenne pepper

Mix all the devilled butter ingredients together. This will keep, chilled, for ages.

In a heavy sauté pan melt 110g devilled butter and gently fry the shallots until soft. Add the kidneys and fry gently until cooked (they should be pink) – about 5 minutes.

Serve on toast.

Smoked haddock with black pudding

This is more a breakfast combination than a recipe and came about following my stay at the Marcliffe at Pitfodels, Stuart Soence's brilliant Aberdeen hotel. The quality of their smoked haddock was outstanding – nice fat fish, well smoked – but they also served Charlie Barley's delicious black pudding from Stornaway, made with sheep's blood. During my rectorship of the university I used to stay at the Marcliffe, but usually only for one or two nights at a time. One morning, riven with indecision, I decided to order both and was delighted to discover how well they went together. As I love both smoked haddock and black pudding, this has become a regular breakfast or supper dish for me. This recipe serves two – of course, for me, more than two at breakfast is de trop.

SERVES 2

4 slices good black pudding

a little bacon fat or oil, for frying

300ml milk

1 large or two smaller pieces smoked haddock

2 eggs

Gently fry your black pudding in the bacon fat or oil. Heat the milk in a large sauté pan, carefully add the haddock and poach gently for a few minutes, until just cooked. Transfer to warm plates.

Poach the eggs – you can do this in the haddock milk if you like, making sure it is deep enough (add a little water if necessary).

Place the eggs on top of the haddock fillets, arrange the slices of black pudding and serve.

Soups

Onion soup with stilton rind

When I get home from rushing around the country, one of the first things I do is to make a huge pot of onion soup. So easy to make and so consoling, whilst I sit staring at the wall with exhaustion. It was my best friend since school – writer and poet Christine Coleman – who had the idea of adding the grated Stilton rind, and it gives the soup a whole different body. Christine was one of eight children so nothing was ever wasted in her house; I have always hated throwing out the remains of the Christmas Stilton, so this is a great way of using it up. I also always like to float a piece of buttered toast on top, covered in sliced mature Cheddar and browned under the grill.

SERVES 6

75g butter

a dash of olive oil (to stop the butter burning)

4 good-sized strong onions, sliced

salt and pepper

300ml strong beef stock (or use stock cube)

1 can or bottle of bitter beer

75g grated Stilton rind

In a large saucepan heat the butter and oil and fry the onion slices gently until golden. If you like a very dark onion soup (I don't personally), fry them longer until they are caramelised. Season. Add the stock and the beer and bring to the boil. Partially cover and leave to simmer for 1 hour.

Adjust the seasoning and add more stock if necessary. Add the rind and cook for a further 10 minutes. Decide whether you want the toast on top or just eat with good bread.

Onion, aniseed and tomato soup

This is a soup I came across in Quercy when I was dallying there in my youth, delighted by the dark eyes of a handsome young man. It is a good soup for spring and autumn, although in Quercy it is drunk during the tomato season. Their idea of cool summer nights was never mine.

SERVES 4

4 onions, sliced

2 tablespoons butter

2 garlic cloves, chopped

750g tomatoes, peeled

750ml white/chicken stock

1 bay leaf

3 sprigs thyme

salt and pepper

½ teaspoon aniseed grains

stale sourdough

Sauté the onions in the butter until they are golden. Add the garlic and the tomatoes and cook a little longer. Add the stock and herbs, season and stir in the aniseed. Bring to the boil and simmer for about 1 hour.

Place some slices of stale sourdough bread in the bottom of a tureen, or a round into the bottom of each individual bowl, then pour over the soup and serve.

Chicken soup with dumplings

This is of course the ultimate comfort food – 'Jewish penicillin' we used to call it, to honour the fact that the Jews make the best chicken soup. The difficulty lies nowadays in finding a proper boiling fowl. When I was young, a chicken that was past laying would be knocked on the head, probably at about two or three years old, and used to make the most delicious broth. Today, eating chickens are killed at five weeks unless you are very lucky and get one that's nine weeks old. My friend, Linda Dick, kills them at between eleven and fifteen and the difference is noticeable. It is not always nostalgia that creates a memory of better things; some things just were better. Should you ever have a chance to taste it I'm sure you will agree I'm right. Sometimes I find an old hen in a Chinese supermarket, but I wonder as I look at free-range egg producers what they do with their old layers? To compensate the defect, the best thing to do is to add a veal knuckle or a pig's trotter along with your chicken. The best and lightest dumplings are made with chicken fat, and before you ask me where you buy it, you don't. If you buy decent chickens you will find lumps of lovely yellow fat within the breast cavity. Cook these gently in a pan and they will render up a bowl of delicious chicken fat, which keeps well in a dish in the fridge.

SERVES 4

1 chicken

1 veal knuckle or pig's trotter

1 onion, roughly chopped

2 carrots

2 stalks celery

salt and 6 crunched peppercorns

FOR THE DUMPLINGS

175g fresh white breadcrumbs

75g chicken fat or beef suet

2 tablespoons parsley, finely chopped

grated zest of 1 lemon

salt and pepper

1–2 eggs

Fill a large pan with water and simmer the chicken and other stock ingredients for 2–3 hours until the broth is good and strong. Strain, remove the chicken flesh from the carcass and give it to the dog (unless it is a proper boiling fowl, in which case, slice the flesh to add to the soup).

For the dumplings, mix together all the ingredients except the eggs. Lightly beat the eggs then add to the other ingredients and mix well. Add spoonfuls of the mixture to the soup for the last 15–20 minutes of cooking time.

Chestnut soup

I love this soup, and now that we can buy ready packed chestnuts to bulk out those we have patiently peeled ourselves, it is all the easier! My friend Germain de Marques (whose restaurant is just outside Stockbridge in Hampshire) introduced me to the idea of adding the liver, which carries the soup to another dimension, but it is still excellent without. The truffled cream is also his idea but ordinary cream is good too. It is a most comforting soup on a cold winter's night.

SERVES 4

500g peeled chestnuts

pheasant stock

salt and pepper

100g goose or duck liver, chopped

50g butter

2 medium onions, chopped

125ml cream

a few drops truffle oil

Cook the chestnuts in 600ml stock until they are soft and falling to pieces. Purée them in a blender, then return them to the pan and add more stock so that the soup is not too thick. Season.

Sauté the onions in the butter, add the chopped liver, but don't overcook it.

When you are ready to serve the soup, add the liver and cook for a few minutes to heat through. Whip the cream and add the truffle oil. Float a spoonful on top of each bowl of soup before serving.

Seafood and coconut soup

This is one of my easiest and favourite lunch dishes. Use any fish that takes your fancy; I simply nip down to my wonderful fishmonger Davy Clarke and buy what ever appeals: hake, conger eel, salmon, even fillets of sole or plaice, adjusting cooking times to suit and adding them at different times. To make a more robust dish, cook some egg noodles separately and add them to the soup at the last minute.

SERVES 2

1 tablespoon olive oil

1 tablespoon sesame oil

6 spring onions, chopped

thumb-sized piece root ginger, finely chopped

1 chilli (whatever strength you like), chopped

6 peeled raw prawns

½ teaspoon blachan (shrimp paste), optional

1 x 400g tin coconut milk

150ml fish stock

good handful squid rings or small squid

piece of white fish, about 100g

dash of soy sauce

Heat the oils in a saucepan, add the spring onions, ginger and chilli and fry gently. Add the prawns and fry for 2–3 minutes. Add the blachan (if using) and dissolve into the mixture. Pour in the coconut milk and the stock and bring to the boil. Add the squid and the fish and simmer for about 5–10 minutes until the fish is cooked. (If using fillets of plaice or sole they will need only 2 or 3 minutes to cook through, so add them later.) Add soy sauce, taste and serve.

Parsnip and crab soup

This recipe is my friend Sue Lawrence's, from her first book 'Entertaining at Home in Scotland'. I first met Sue when she was signing this book at Books for Cooks in London, and she brought this delicious soup for the punters to taste. I fell in love with it, and I subsequently included it in my list of the ten best things I have ever eaten, published in 'Country Life'.

SERVES 4

2 tablespoons olive oil

1 onion

2 garlic cloves, chopped

2 celery sticks, chopped

2 heaped teaspoons ground cumin

600g parsnips, chopped

1.2 litres chicken stock

50ml Noilly Pratt

salt and pepper

175g crabmeat

1 tablespoon extra-virgin olive oil

Heat the oil in a large pan and fry the onion, garlic and celery for 10 minutes. Add the cumin and cook, stirring well, for 30 seconds. Add the parsnips, stir well to coat them with fat and cook for another 5 minutes. Add the hot stock and bring to the boil. Cover, reduce the heat to a simmer and cook for a further 25 minutes or until the vegetables are tender.

Blend or liquidise in batches with the Noilly Prat. Adjust the seasoning to taste.

Mix the crabmeat with the olive oil and season, then float a spoonful of this mixture on top of each bowl of soup before serving.

Cucumber soup

In the 1950s, my mother was sent Vincent Price's cookery book from America, and in it was a recipe for cold cucumber soup – very avant-garde at that time and served at summer lunches. Cooked cucumbers were a regular visitor to 19th century tables and I often serve them. Nowadays, they seem only to emerge in salads or with yogurt. I suspect the new, straight, burpless, unbitter varieties are the reason for this.

SERVES 4

25g butter

50g onion, chopped

1 large cucumber

15g plain flour

600ml chicken stock

zest and juice of ½ lemon

salt and pepper

250ml single cream

1 dessertspoon chopped mint

Melt the butter in a saucepan and sauté the onion until soft but not coloured. Peel and deseed the cucumbers and cut into cubes and add to the onions. Cover and cook until the cucumber is cooked, but not soft. Remove the lid and allow the steam to escape, then sprinkle on the flour. Stir in the stock and cook for 15 minutes.

Blend the soup, add the lemon juice and zest and season to taste. Add the cream but do not allow it to boil. Remove from the heat, leave to cool, then refrigerate.

Stir in the chopped mint just before serving.

Rice soup

Rice is always comforting, soothing and good for the digestion. The rice congees that the Chinese eat for lunch are too reminiscent of the gruel I ate in my period as a sickly child for my liking, but this recipe is slightly more robust, whilst still retaining the comfort factor. It is a meal in one.

SERVES 4

3 tablespoons olive oil

3 spring onions, thinly sliced

4 garlic cloves, thinly sliced

1 small chilli, chopped

handful of coriander leaves

225g lean pork, finely chopped

6 raw king prawns, peeled and cut in half

2 teaspoons palm sugar or light brown sugar

900ml white stock

225g cooked rice

2 tablespoons asian fish sauce

1 tablespoon oyster sauce

Heat the oil in a pan and fry the spring onions, garlic, chilli and half the coriander leaves. Add the pork and prawns and cook until the prawns change colour. Stir in the sugar and cook for a little longer. Pour off the surplus oil and add the rice, stock and other ingredients. Cook for a further 15 minutes. If liked, add a couple of lightly whisked eggs into the mixture and stir vigorously.

Starters

Potted crab

The easiest and most delicious of starters. If you don't want to pick over your crab, buy a fresh dressed one. Frozen or tinned will also do for this dish.

SERVES 4

25g butter per crab

1 dressed crab per person (or 100g crabmeat, both white and brown if possible)

½ teaspoon nutmeg

½ teaspoon cayenne pepper

salt and pepper

juice of 1 lemon

Melt the butter in a large sauté pan and stir in the crabmeat. Add all the other ingredients except the lemon juice, adjusting the seasoning to taste. Cook gently until all the butter is melded in. At the last minute, stir in the lemon juice and serve warm with toast.

Salt cod and tomatoes

I really only discovered salt cod when I was sailing in the Caribbean. A West Indian staple and, originally a cheap preservable slave food, it is to be found in the islands in many forms. This recipe – a lovely starter, main course salad or lunchtime snack – is the invention of my sexy Swedish photographer friend Carin, and I love it. Salt fish needs to be soaked overnight in cold water to both remove the excess salt and plump it up a bit.

SERVES 4

175–225g piece salt cod, soaked overnight

olive oil

1 onion, finely chopped

1 small garlic clove, chopped

1 small chilli, chopped (optional)

6 tomatoes skinned, deseeded and chopped

lemon or lime juice

salt and pepper

Cook your fish gently in a little water for about 10 minutes until it is ready to come away from the skin. Drain, remove the skin and bones, then flake it into a bowl.

In a little oil, gently fry the onion, garlic and chilli, if used, then add to the fish, followed by the tomatoes.

Make a dressing with oil and the lime or lemon juice and mix into the fish. Eat cold.

Elly's lattice

I invented this as the last dish I typed up for this book. It is dedicated to Elly James, assistant to my dear agent Heather Holden-Brown. Without Elly's support, encouragement and gift of laughter, I would never have finished this book. It includes some of her favourite ingredients, and comes with my thanks.

SERVES 4

450g shortcrust pastry

1 dessertspoon olive oil

1 garlic clove, mashed

2 anchovy fillets

10 king prawns, peeled

175g wilted spinach

3 rashers streaky bacon, chopped and fried

110g baby broad beans

salt and pepper

beaten egg for glazing

Preheat the oven to 220ºC/425ºF/gas mark 7.

Roll out the pastry into an oblong, cut in half and chill in the fridge.

In a pan, heat the oil, add the garlic and the anchovies and cook until the fillets melt. Add the prawns and cook until pink, then cut into bite-sized pieces and season. Stir in the spinach and bacon. Blanch the broad beans in a little salted boiling water for 3–4 minutes. Drain, and add to the prawn and spinach mixture.

Place one half of the pastry on a lightly greased oven sheet. Spread the prawn filling onto the pastry, leaving a 2.5cm border around the edge, cover with the other sheet of pastry and seal the edges carefully with a little beaten egg. Cut slashes in the top and glaze with more egg. Cook in the preheated oven until golden – about 25 minutes.

Tomato summer pudding

Every cook has one invented recipe of which they are most proud and this was Jennifer's. The idea came from an Italian bread salad and I envied her this invention. It is perfect with cold meat or fish and I hope you enjoy it as much as I do. The better and riper the tomatoes, the better the pudding.

SERVES 4

olive oil

8–10 slices good white bread, crusts removed

2kg ripe tomatoes, skinned and deseeded

salt and pepper

1 garlic clove, finely chopped

bunch of basil

juice of ½ lemon

Pour some olive oil on a flat dish and dip the bread quickly into it, then use to line a 1.2-litre pudding basin. Chop the tomatoes and pour any remaining oil over them. Season well. Add the garlic and tear the basil leaves into the tomato mixture. Put it into the lined pudding basin and squeeze on the lemon juice. Make a cover with bread and lay in place. Put a flat plate over the pudding and place weights on top to press it down. Leave overnight in the refrigerator.

To serve, run a knife carefully around the outside and turn the pudding out onto a flat dish. Good old Jennifer, delicious.

Mirrored eggs

This dish, from William Verral's cookbook, is an excellent starter or supper dish. He was chef to the Duke of Newcastle and was sent for an exchange to the kitchens of the Marquis de St Cloud. He came back complaining the French only had one sauce! Eventually he became one of the great political taverners of the 18th century, owning the White Hart at Lewes, which numbered among its residents, Tom Paine.

SERVES 4

1 bunch spring onions, chopped

1 small bunch watercress, chopped

6 eggs

300ml double cream

juice of ½ orange and ½ lemon

salt and pepper

a little butter

Preheat the oven to 180ºC/350ºF/gas mark 4.

Butter a shallow ovenproof dish and lay the chopped spring onions and watercress in the bottom. Carefully break the eggs on top. Mix the cream and the citrus juices together and pour over the eggs. Season and dot with a little butter and bake in a bain-marie for 15 minutes, or until the eggs are set.

Drappit eggs with sables

A drappit egg is Scots for a poached egg because you 'drap' or drop it into the water; a sable is a very short cheese biscuit. This recipe well repays the effort.

SERVES 4

FOR THE SABLES

75g butter

75g mature Cheddar, finely grated

110g plain flour

pinch of salt

good pinch of dry mustard powder

FOR THE EGGS

6 eggs

300ml hollandaise or cheese sauce

Preheat the oven to 200ºC/400ºF/gas mark 6. To make the sables, cream the butter, add the cheese and cream again until soft. Mix in the other ingredients and knead to a smooth dough. This can be done in a food-processor but don't overmix. Wrap the dough in clingfilm or greaseproof paper and refrigerate for 30 minutes.

Roll out the dough, cut into squares and bake until golden.

Poach your eggs, drain well, place one on each square and cover with sauce. Serve at once.

Fuzdah's eggs

When my step grandfather Ezeckial Manasseh went from Calcutta to Singapore, his mother sent with him a cook called Fuzdah from the black Jewish community in Cochin. This is one of his specialities which used to be served at breakfast. It was lost when my grandmother died, but Claudia Roden found it for me when she was researching her great book on Jewish food. It is more a brunch or supper dish but I hope you enjoy it as much as I do.

SERVES 4

6 eggs

1 dessertspoon olive oil

1 shallot, minced

small bunch spring onions, chopped

2 garlic cloves, chopped

1 thumb-sized piece of root ginger, sliced into thin strips

2 small chillies, chopped

1 x 400g tin coconut milk

½ teaspoon ground cumin

2 tomatoes, skinned, deseeded and chopped

1 mango, cubed

bunch of coriander

juice of 2 limes

salt and pepper

Hard-boil your eggs for about 10 minutes, then peel.

Heat the oil in a heavy sauté pan and gently fry the minced shallot for about 3 minutes. Add the spring onions, garlic, ginger and chillies. Pour in the coconut milk and simmer until it separates, about 5 minutes. Stir in the ground cumin, then add the hard-boiled eggs, the tomatoes and the mango cubes. Tear in the coriander, add the lime juice and season. Simmer gently for another 5 minutes and serve with rice or naan.

Cheese soufflé

When I first went to work for Rebekka Hardy she said they would just have something simple the first night, like a cheese soufflé. I froze, I had never made a large soufflé before. The only book in the house was Robert Carrier's cookbook in which he had written, 'There is a lot of rubbish talked about the mystique of this dish, if you can make a white sauce you can make a soufflé'. He was, of course, right and I have never looked back – such a comfort, a cheese soufflé.

SERVES 4

100g plain flour

salt

1 teaspoon mustard powder

pinch of cayenne pepper

600ml milk

100g strong Cheddar, grated

4 egg yolks

butter

5 egg whites

1 tablespoon grated Parmesan

Preheat the oven to 220ºC/425ºF/gas mark 7.

In a heavy saucepan make a roux: melt the butter and once it is melted, stir in the flour, mix well and allow to cook for 2–3 minutes. Season and stir in the mustard powder and the cayenne. Gradually add the milk, but each time you add it do not stir the mixture until the milk has reached the temperature of the mixture, then stir vigorously. Stir in the cheese and allow to melt and blend. Remove from the heat, stand for 1 minute, then stir in the egg yolks one by one.

Butter a 2-pint soufflé dish and sprinkle the parmesan on the butter. In a clean bowl, whip the egg whites until stiff – they must form stiff peaks. Using a metal spoon fold the whites into the mixture, mixing well. Pour into the soufflé dish and place in the middle of the preheated oven until well risen and just browning – about 20 minutes. Do not open the oven whilst cooking. Serve at once – the guests must wait for the soufflé not the other way round!

Military pork puffs

When I used to visit my grandmother in Singapore, we would have these delicious savouries made with cold leftover pork and the distinctive flavour of military pickle. Any tangy pickle will do, especially a lemon-based one but Branston is good, too, if you add a dash of lemon. As the meat is already cooked this is baked at one temperature.

SERVES 4

25g butter

1 small onion, chopped

25g flour

150ml stock

4 tablespoons natural yogurt

2 tablespoons pickle

175g cooked pork, finely chopped

salt and pepper

225g puff or flaky pastry

beaten egg, for glazing

Preheat the oven to 220°C/245°F/gas mark 7.

Melt the butter and fry the onion until golden. Add the flour, stir in the stock and cook for a few minutes more. Stir in the yogurt, pickle and pork and season well. Leave to cool.

Roll out one third of the pastry and cut into four 12.5cm circles. Place on a lightly greased baking sheet and spoon on the filling, leaving a margin of 1cm. Roll out the remaining pastry and cut into 4 rounds slightly larger than the first lot. Place these over the top of the filled rounds, damp the edges press firmly and scallop the edges. Cut a small hole in the centre of each (to let the steam escape), decorate with pastry trimmings and glaze with beaten egg.

Bake for 30–35 minutes until well risen and golden. Serve hot or cold.

Potato cake with ham and cheese

This is a really comforting savoury snack for a winter's afternoon.

SERVES 4

6 medium potatoes, peeled and sliced

4 slices ham

2 tablespoons lard

200g Cheddar cheese, grated

pepper

Preheat the oven to 180°C/350°F/gas mark 4.

Dry the sliced potatoes. De-rind the ham and cut into strips.

Melt the lard in a heavy, ovenproof pan, add the ham strips and cook until softened. Remove two-thirds. Add the potatoes in layers, interspersing with the removed ham, cheese and pepper. Cook until you think the bottom is browned – about 10 minutes.

Then place in the oven for an hour. Turn out onto a plate by inverting the pan – it will be a golden cake.

Salads

Artichoke hearts with parma ham

This is a very successful salad for a summer lunch. Without the ham it becomes merely a side dish, but otherwise this salad makes for a filling dish.

Do try to grow your own rocket. It calls for very little space and tastes infinitely superior to even the so-called 'wild' rocket in shops – much more flavour with a delicious bitter edge. Its growth gives rocket its name – it shoots up like a rocket – and you have to be quick to pick it, so it will grow some more. If you do not grow your own artichokes, you can buy perfectly good hearts in delicatessens, preserved in oil. I am not usually a fan of balsamic vinegar, which has become very fashionable with chefs. However, it goes well here. Buy the oldest balsamic you can afford and use it sparingly. I have a small bottle of 90-year-old balsamic which has lasted me for 15 years so far! This is a layered salad and one that you can make in advance as everything keeps.

SERVES 4

10 artichoke hearts, cut into thirds

5 slices Parma ham

lots of rocket

FOR THE DRESSING

olive oil (from the artichoke jar if using bottled hearts)

balsamic vinegar

juice of ½ a lemon

salt and pepper

In a flattish salad dish, place the hearts, ham and rocket in layers.

Make a dressing with olive oil, a small amount of balsamic (enough to taste), lemon juice and seasoning. Pour over the salad 10 minutes before serving and mix carefully.

Crab with pine nuts

This dish is straight out of Patrick Lamb, a chef who wrote in the 17th century, yet it could be from any of the new-wave American chefs of the 1980s.

I love crab – the first thing I ever cooked was crab in a galvanised bucket on the beach, aged ten. Curiously, it was also one of the things I cooked in the very first 'Two Fat Ladies' programme.

There is an awful lot of rubbish spoken about the 'poisonous' bits of a crab, but the dead men's fingers are the only inedible bit, and no one would think of eating these fibrous, finger-shaped bits of the crab's interior. For this dish, you want white crabmeat – it is much nicer fresh than frozen or tinned, but the choice is down to you. An easy option is to buy a dressed crab and remove the white meat.

SERVES 4

225g white crabmeat

1 tablespoon pine nuts, lightly roasted

small piece of root ginger

FOR THE DRESSING

yolks of 2 hard-boiled eggs

salt and pepper

olive oil

juice of 2 oranges

Put the crabmeat in a bowl. Smash the pine nuts into smallish pieces, then mix with the crabmeat. Cut the ginger into very fine strips and mix in with the crabs.

Mash the egg yolks in a bowl and season with salt and pepper. Slowly pour in the olive oil, stirring as you go to form an emulsified dressing. Add the orange juice.

Pour the dressing over the crab mixture, mix well and adjust the seasoning to taste.

Aubergine and smoked tofu

'What?' I hear you cry. 'Clarissa and tofu?' But you must remember that I am an omnivore, and it is from that perspective that I object to vegetarians – they are missing so much of the picture. One told me the other day that he would have no objection to eating a deer that had been run down by men with spears; my feeling is both men and deer would prefer the progression to a rifle. The only bit we agreed on was that it should be eaten! But I do love tofu, as my real comfort food is Chinese (I expect I was Chinese in a previous life).

I invented this dish for my friend Alice Klouda who, being a direct descendant of Queen Victoria's father, had that horrid, metabolic disease porphyria, and found herself restricted in mid-life to a vegan diet.

SERVES 4

1 aubergine

2 tablespoons olive oil

1 garlic clove, chopped

6 spring onions, chopped

bunch of coriander

1 chilli, finely chopped

175g smoked tofu

1 x 400g tin tomatoes

salt and pepper

Cut the aubergine into 1cm cubes. In a large saucepan, heat the olive oil and fry the chopped garlic. Add the aubergine pieces, tossing them in the oil. Add the spring onions, half the coriander, roughly chopped, and the chilli.

Cut the tofu into 2.5cm cubes and add to the pan, mixing well. Pour on the tomatoes and season very well. Cover and cook for about 15 minutes or until the aubergine is done, stirring from time to time. Serve with rice.

Jerusalem artichokes and prawns

Jerusalem artichokes are such a reassuring vegetable to grow. I once grew 20kg of them in a tiny bed in Battersea that would welcome nothing else! They are not artichokes at all, nor indeed anything to do with that city which the 'People of the Book' – as the Muslims refer to Jews and Christians (the book being the Bible) – have fought over for the whole of post-Roman history. They are, in fact, members of the sunflower family. A sunflower is called girasole in Italian and, with the English habit of corrupting the names imposed on us by foreign invaders, it has become 'Jerusalem'. And why artichoke? Because they taste like artichoke heart. I think my mother adapted this recipe from one by Elizabeth David, whom she was a great fan, but it is hard to follow my mother's thought processes. Jerusalem artichokes are hard to clean and peel, so soak them in cold water for an hour before attempting to wash them. I tend to cook them before peeling as this is a lot easier.

SERVES 4

10 Jerusalem artichokes	2 garlic cloves
lemon juice	6 large prawns, peeled
3–4 tomatoes, peeled, deseeded and chopped	½ teaspoon mustard powder
olive oil	salt and pepper
	½ teaspoon pickled lemon

Gently cook the artichokes in salted water until they are cooked but not soft. Plunge them into cold water, then peel and slice them. Put them in a salad bowl and sprinkle with lemon juice to stop them discolouring. Mix in the tomatoes.

Heat a pan and put in the olive oil. Chop one of the garlic cloves into this and add the prawns, frying until they are cooked, about 6–10 minutes. Chop the prawns into small pieces and add to the artichokes.

Mash the other garlic clove with a little salt. Use this to make a dressing along with the mustard powder, salt and pepper and either lemon juice or white wine vinegar. Chop the pickled lemon and stir it in with the artichokes, then mix in the dressing. This dish tastes delicious served with bread or a green salad.

Noodles, pasta & rice

My Chinese noodles

Mostly, I prefer noodles to pasta. A Chinese friend once told me that most Chinese buy 'Dolly' noodles to eat at home. This brand is readily available in Chinese supermarkets, but if you can't get them use egg noodles. When I am at home, I am a great one for cooking joints of meat for my friends to enjoy, so there is always leftover meat. You can use any cold meat for this, but I prefer pork. The blachan (shrimp paste) and beansprouts are optional.

SERVES 2

1 dessertspoon olive oil

a thumb-sized piece of root ginger, peeled and cut into strips

1 bunch spring onions, chopped

1 chilli, chopped

small piece of blachan (shrimp paste), optional

175–225g diced cold pork, cut into 2.5cm squares

1 dessertspoon sesame oil

1 dessertspoon soy sauce

2 handfuls beansprouts (optional)

2 packets Dolly noodles or 1 packet egg noodles

Heat the olive oil in a heavy pan and fry the ginger and spring onions until they become soft. Add the chilli. Crumble in the piece of blachan and add the pork. Mix well and add the sesame oil and soy sauce and the beansprouts, if using. Cook for about 5 minutes in which time you should cook the noodles.

Drain the noodles and stir into the pork mixture, mixing well. Allow to cook for another 2–3 minutes and serve.

Scrambled eggs with prawns and cucumber

This is an excellent lunch or supper dish which I came across in Singapore. To bulk it out you can have it with rice or noodles.

SERVES 4

packet of noodles or 250g rice

50g butter

2 garlic cloves, chopped

10 king prawns, peeled

1 tablespoon Asian fish sauce

a dash soy sauce

1 cucumber, cut into 2.5cm pieces

Szechuan or white pepper

4 eggs

Cook the noodles or rice as per packet instructions.

Heat the butter in a heavy pan and fry the garlic. Add the prawns and cook until they begin to turn pink. Add the fish sauce and the soy sauce and cook for a few minutes. Add the cucumber and some crushed Szechuan pepper or white pepper.

Lightly beat the eggs in a bowl and add a pinch of salt. Fold the eggs into the prawns, stirring as you go, and serve.

Spaghetti with botargo

When I was a child my father used to eat botargo, the dried mullet roe so beloved of Mediterranean countries. I thought it was horrid, but now I am grown up I love it too. At VinCaffè, Francesca Contini's delightful cafe next to Harvey Nichols in Edinburgh, they serve this simple but delicious dish. The Italians don't eat Parmesan with fish – a chef called Anacleto once threw a knife at my head for asking for it with vongole – but I am not Italian, and by and large they humour me.

SERVES 4

200g spaghetti or spaghettini

olive oil

2 garlic cloves, thinly sliced

25g botargo, crumbled

Parmesan cheese

Cook the pasta in lots of water in a big pan (this gets the starch out). Meanwhile, heat some olive oil in a pan and gently fry the garlic.

When the pasta is ready, drain it and stir in a spoonful of olive oil to prevent it sticking. Transfer to a dish, then mix in the garlic and its oil and stir in the crumbled botargo. Add Parmesan if you are a Philistine like me!

Lamb with yogurt

This is an adaptation of an Iranian recipe that the great Sri Owen included in her award-winning 'The Rice Book'. I am a huge admirer of Sri, and her recipe is infinitely more interesting than mine, but this is a comfort book and when it comes to comfort, simplicity is all.

SERVES 4

FOR THE MARINADE

3 garlic cloves

2 shallots

½ teaspoon cinnamon

1 teaspoon salt

½ teaspoon cayenne pepper

225ml plain yogurt

10 lamb cutlets

olive oil

450g Basmati or long-grain rice

butter

salt and pepper

Blend all the marinade ingredients except the yogurt in a food processor. Stir the mixture into the yogurt, then pour over the cutlets. Leave in a cool place overnight (rather than a fridge).

Preheat the oven to 180°C/350°F/gas mark 4.

Shake the marinade off the lamb (set aside the marinade for later). Heat the olive oil in a pan, then brown the meat all over.

Cook the rice in boiling salted water for about 8 minutes, drain and rinse under cold water. Mix half the rice with the marinade.

Butter a flameproof casserole or oven dish lavishly and spread the mixed rice over the bottom. Place the cutlets on top and then the remaining rice over them, seasoning as you go. Cover and cook for about 1 hour.

Kedgeree

I often think of the Memsahib who invented kedgeree. Was she poor and making ends meet? Was her husband a tyrant, or did she do it to please? Or was she just bored? Whatever the story, we owe her a debt of gratitude. I tend to make my kedgeree with smoked haddock and keep it simple, but here I have used cooked salmon, which needs a bit more flavour. Kedgeree originated from the Indian 'khichiri', a dish of rice and lentils, and the recipe I have given is more in keeping with that. It is a great dish whatever way you prepare it. To bulk out the recipe you can add cauliflower or potatoes.

SERVES 8

1 teaspoon coriander seeds

½ teaspoon cardamom seeds

1 tablespoon ground turmeric

1 teaspoon cayenne pepper

1 dried red chilli

4 tablespoons ghee or clarified butter

1 onion, ½ chopped, ½ slivered

500g long-grain rice

500g brown lentils

salt

500g cooked salmon, flaked

4 hard-boiled eggs, shelled and cut into quarters

1 tablespoon vegetable oil

1 tablespoon slivered almonds

coriander, to garnish

Pound the spices and chilli together. Put them in a saucepan with 1.2 litres water and simmer for 10 minutes. Strain and keep the water.

In a large saucepan, melt the ghee or butter and fry the chopped onion until coloured. Add the rice and lentils and cook, stirring continuously, for 2 minutes. Add the strained spice water and the salt and simmer until all the moisture has been absorbed and all is cooked and tender. Stir in the cooked fish carefully, along with the hard-boiled eggs.

Heat the oil in a separate pan and fry the onion slivers until brown and crisp, then drain well on kitchen paper. Sauté the almonds quickly in the same pan. Turn the kedgeree onto a serving dish and scatter the onions and almonds on top. Garnish with coriander. Serve as is, or with a curry sauce if liked.

Paella

Spain abounds with paella-type recipes, using the local ingredients of the region in question. This one is a great party dish and easy to cook for big numbers.

SERVES 4–6

5 tablespoons olive oil

1 whole chicken, cut into pieces

600g raw prawns

3 garlic cloves, finely chopped

100g jamón Iberico (or other serrano ham)

100g chorizo, cubed

24 mussels, shelled

500g risotto or paella rice

½ teaspoon paprika

pinch of cayenne pepper

small tin tomato purée

salt and pepper

1 sachet saffron threads

1.2 litres white stock

200ml white wine

125g frozen peas

2 red peppers, roasted and skinned (or 1 small tin)

In a paella pan or a large flat pan, heat the oil and brown the chicken pieces. Add the prawns and garlic and fry gently for a couple of minutes. Add the ham, chorizo and mussels, then add the rice, paprika, cayenne and tomato purée. Season and stir well.

Soften the saffron strands in a little warm stock and add to the dish. Pour on the wine and half the stock. When the rice has absorbed the liquid, add more stock. Continue to cook gently over the heat for 30 minutes or until the chicken is cooked, adding the peas after 25 minutes. Alternatively, cook in the oven on 180ºC/350ºF/gas mark 4 for 40 minutes. Serve garnished with strips of red pepper.

Fish

Fish pie

What nicer dish to eat by your fire in winter or share with friends outside on a spring or autumn evening with a soft woollen cardigan to keep out the cool. Wear wool as man-made fibres aren't comforting and destroy the planet. Moreover, as we are all turning down our washing machines to 30 degrees you will have no trouble washing such garments. However, you don't want your fish pie to resemble wool in any way so don't overcook your fish!

25g butter

25g flour

425ml whole milk

1 dessertspoon dry sherry

little olive oil or butter

2 onions, chopped

1 garlic clove, chopped

250g spinach, washed

3 springs of lemon balm (*Melissa*), optional

900g fish (a mix of e.g. haddock, cod, smoked haddock, conger eel)

12 large prawns, raw, peeled and cut in half

3 hard-boiled eggs, quartered

bunch of parsley (curly), chopped

6 large potatoes, boiled and mashed

50g grated Cheddar

Make a roux with the butter and flour, then add the milk and sherry to form a fairly thick white sauce.

Preheat the oven to 150ºC/350ºF/gas mark 4.

In a little olive oil or butter, fry the onions and garlic until soft. Put the spinach and the lemon balm in the bottom of your pie dish, followed by the onions and garlic. Arrange the fish, cut into pieces, and prawns on top along with the hard-boiled eggs. Pour over the sauce. Scatter the parsley on top of the fish, season and cover with the mashed potato. Make patterns on the potatoes with a fork, then sprinkle on the grated cheese and bake in the oven for 45 minutes. When it is cooked, the top should be nice and brown; if not, flash under a grill.

Coconut mackerel

This is an adaptation of a dish by that very good Indian cook Anjum Anand, whose first series was the only cookery programme I watched in 2007. She chooses to describe herself as a chef but I would pay her the compliment of calling her a cook.

If you fish for mackerel – which is really the only way to eat them – you usually have a lot and this is a very good way of using them.

SERVES 4

1 dessertspoon olive oil

2 shallots, minced

2 small chillies, chopped

1 garlic clove, mashed with some salt

1 x 400g tin coconut milk

2 teaspoons fenugreek seeds

2 teaspoons curry powder

1½ mackerel per person, boned and cut lengthways into 2 fillets

salt and pepper

In a large, heavy frying pan heat the oil and fry the shallots until they change colour. Add the chillies and the mashed garlic and cook a little longer. Pour in the coconut milk and cook for about 5 minutes, until the milk splits and then thickens. Stir in the fenugreek seeds and the curry powder and cook for a couple more minutes. Place each mackerel fillet, skin-side down, in the mixture and allow to cook through – about 5–10 minutes. Do not overcook. Season. Unless the mackerel are very large you shouldn't need to turn them, but spoon the hot liquid over the top.

Serve with rice and/or a green salad.

Salt cod with prunes

All over the Catholic countries of Europe, fish is eaten on Christmas Eve, a day of fasting and abstinence, and in the land-locked areas this is most often salt cod. I have eaten this dish many times at Valvona and Crolla; it is Philip Contini's (mine host) favourite dish and Mary has given me the recipe. The prunes should be plump and stoned; if dried, soak in advance.

SERVES 2

1 piece salt cod, about 175g

olive oil

1 onion, chopped

1 garlic clove, chopped

1 x 400g tin tomatoes

8 prunes

salt and pepper

Soak the cod overnight, then cook in a little water until you can remove the skin and bones. Heat some olive oil in a pan and fry the onion until soft, but not coloured. Add the garlic and cook a little more. Put the cod on top of the onions and then pour on the tomatoes. Add the prunes and seasoning.

Poach the fish gently in the tomatoes for about 30 minutes or until cooked. Serve with boiled potatoes.

Fish stew

Choose your favourite fish to put in this delightfully simple stew. A great alternative to fish pie.

SERVES 4

2 tablespoons olive oil

2 medium onions, peeled and chopped

2 garlic cloves, chopped

1 small tin anchovies

4 tomatoes, chopped (or 1 x 400g tin)

300ml fish stock or white wine

2 medium potatoes, cut into chunks

700g fish – salmon, hake, cod, grey mullet, coley, conger eel or whatever

8 prawns, peeled

2 teaspoons capers or caperberries, chopped

2 tablespoons dry sherry

salt and pepper

In a large pan heat the oil and fry the onions until soft. Add the garlic and the anchovies and allow the latter to melt in to the oil. Add the tomatoes, stock or white wine and potatoes, and cook gently for about 10 minutes. The sauce will reduce a little.

Add the more solid fish and the prawns and cook gently for 5 minutes. Add the softer fish, the capers and the sherry. Cook for a further 5 minutes until all the fish is cooked. If it appears to get dry, add a little more liquid.

Eat with good bread or possibly salad if the season is right.

Roast conger eel

Conger eel is a much-ignored fish, except among the West Indian community. I love its texture and meaty flavour. When we were filming 'Clarissa and the Countryman', Tug, Johnny's terrier, caught a conger eel and we barbecued it – and very good it was, too. I also put eel in fish pies, for variation. This West Country dish uses cider to cut the possible glutinous liquid.

SERVES 4

1 whole middle-cut conger eel (30–45cm), cleaned and dried

1 onion, cut in half for the rubbing, then chopped for the stuffing

mustard powder

450g sausage meat

thyme

salt and pepper

1 apple, halved

50g beef dripping

300ml dry cider

Preheat the oven to 180°C/350°F/gas mark 4.

Rub the inside of the eel with the onion, then wipe with a little mustard powder. Make a stuffing with the sausage meat, chopped onion, thyme and seasoning – it should be tasty! Stuff the eel and plug each end with half an apple, pushing them well in as they will be forced out by the cooking.

Push a long skewer through the apples, tie up with string and put in a roasting pan. Smear the dripping over the eel and pour on the cider. Cover with foil as it splutters badly, then cook in the oven for between 45 minutes and 1 hour, depending on the size of the fish. Baste throughout cooking.

Eels in herbs, Brussels-style

When I was a child, every London fishmonger kept a tank of live eels. Either they would kill and skin them for you or you would take it home alive and keep them until you were ready. The gardener would kill our eels, nail them to the potting shed door, then skin them. When I was a young barrister we would go to the riverside pubs at Hammersmith and Chiswick, where the rough boys fished the Thames for eels and I would buy one for a few shillings to take home. As a Londoner, I love jellied eels and one of the great joys of Derby day was going across the course to the downs side and buying jellied eels from the whelk stalls. In Kent and Sussex, the farmers used to refer to eels as the gentlemen who paid the rent, as a well stocked marsh was a valuable asset. Today it is very hard to buy a live eel, or even a dead one come to that, but they are easy enough to catch for yourself; or, if you know a water bailiff, they will often sell you one.

The Northern Irish eel fishermen on Loch Beg throw the whole eel into a pan with some bacon fat and fry it for breakfast and eat it with soda bread farls – delicious.

All you need to catch one is a bit of meat that is over-ripe on a hook or, if you own a bit of water, sink an eel trap. Nowadays, most eels are sent to Holland for smoking or even smoked in the UK. The best smoked eel I ever ate was cured by a Lithuanian, but it is a pity not to try fresh eel. The Chinese do it beautifully with black bean sauce, but my favourite was cooked in Brussels by the chef of a step-great aunt whose measurement around her waist when she was married was the same as that around her neck when she died, aged ninety-four. She was hale and hardworking to the end and died very suddenly. Aunt Emmy was reputed to have the best chef in Brussels (no small boast as Belgian food is fantastic). The funeral feast was incredible and this is one of the dishes we ate.

SERVES 4

75g butter

2 tablespoons onion, finely chopped

2 tablespoons green celery leaves, finely chopped

1.3kg eels, skinned, washed and cut into the same-size pieces

1 glass dry white wine

small pinch of ground cloves

4 tablespoons finely chopped watercress

small pinch of thyme

4 tablespoons finely chopped sorrel leaves

1 tablespoon finely chopped parsley

1 tablespoon finely chopped chervil

3 tablespoons finely chopped white nettle leaves

1 teaspoon finely chopped sage

1 teaspoon finely chopped summer savory

1 teaspoon finely chopped mint

125ml double cream

4 egg yolks

salt and pepper

In a frying pan, melt the butter and fry the onion and celery leaves until the onion becomes translucent. Add the fish and fry gently, adding the white wine to moisten. Stir in the ground cloves, the watercress and all the herbs and cook for about 15 minutes. Remove from the heat.

Scald the cream and beat in the egg yolks. Stir into the eel mixture and season.

Serve hot or cold.

Salmon fishcakes

I have always found fish cakes awfully bland. The average one is a blend of fish and potato with little flavour. But then, I thought why am I doing this – you can put other things in as well. Since then, I have used smoked fish, laverbread, chopped hard-boiled eggs, chopped capers and spring onions to liven up my fishcakes. I am particularly fond of using half Irish potato and half sweet potato to avoid the gluey effect, and there is of course Jane Grigson's fishcake in 'Good Things', which is bound with a white sauce.

MAKES ABOUT 16

250g potatoes, chopped into large chunks

250g sweet potatoes, chopped into large chunks

500g cooked salmon, flaked

1 bunch of spring onions, finely chopped

salt and freshly ground black pepper

vegetable oil for frying

Boil the potatoes, drain and mash well. If you are using white, sweet potatoes rather than the red ones, they will take twice as long to cook as an Irish potato.

Mix together the mashed potato with everything else, except the oil, all of which can be done in a food processor. Form into small cakes about the size of half a scone and chill for 30 minutes.

Fry the fishcakes in hot oil until golden brown. They can be cooked in the oven but are never so good. Fishcakes freeze well.

Salmon fishcakes made with gnocchi

This is a dish I invented one day when I had some delicious cold salmon (caught in a haaf-net on the Nith) and some leftover gnocchi and decided to make some fishcakes. I preferred the texture to the usual mash used in fishcakes – I hope you enjoy them, too. And don't worry, you can use commercial gnocchi for this, which has, helpfully, already been mixed with eggs and flour.

SERVES 4

175g cooked gnocchi

225g cooked salmon

4 spring onions

1 egg

olive oil

salt and pepper

Reboil your gnocchi until they float, then drain and roughly mash them (you want to keep some texture). Flake the salmon and finely chop the spring onions. Using your hands, mix all the ingredients except the oil together in a bowl and season well. Form into patties.

Heat the oil in a heavy pan and fry the patties until golden brown: don't turn them until they are cooked on the first side.

Bute herrings

This cold dish is excellent for a buffet meal or lunch on a warm day. The Isle of Bute was always known for the quality of its herrings, which were known as 'magistrates' because of their size and fatness!

This dish takes a little time and attention but is well worth the effort.

SERVES 4

8 herrings

18g salt

75g granulated sugar

450ml cold water

juice of 1 lemon

700g new potatoes

3 eggs

crushed herbs (parsley, thyme, chervil, whatever you will)

125ml salad dressing made with olive oil, vinegar, mustard powder, salt, pepper and a pinch of sugar

Clean and bone the herrings, remove the heads and lay on a flat dish. Sprinkle with the salt and then the sugar. Leave for 4 hours in the fridge or a cool place, then drain and dry thoroughly. You will be amazed at the amount of oil they give up.

Preheat the oven to 180ºC/350ºF/gas mark 4.

Roll up the herrings loosely, with the skin on the outside, and place in an ovenproof dish. Pour over the water and the lemon juice. Cover and bake for 50 minutes.

Meanwhile, boil the new potatoes and hard-boil the eggs. Chop two of the eggs and slice the other. Dice the cooked potatoes and mix with the chopped eggs, herbs and salad dressing to moisten. Remove the herring rolls from the oven, leave to cool then refrigerate.

Lay the herrings on a dish and pack the potato mixture around them. Garnish with chopped parsley and hard-boiled egg slices.

Oyster ateletes

This delicious little dish combines two of my favourite things: oysters and sweetbreads. It was, I believe, a staple of the Paris bordellos, giving extra umph to failing punters. I have never been a failing punter, but it is certainly very invigorating. Obviously, use rock oysters rather than natives, which are too good to do anything with but eat raw.

SERVES 6

32 large oysters

4 sweetbreads

225g bacon rashers

25g parsley, finely chopped

100g shallots, finely chopped

½ teaspoon dried thyme

salt and pepper

1 egg, beaten

50g white breadcrumbs

oil for frying

dry sherry

a dash of Tabasco

Remove the oysters from their shells and set aside the liquid. Cut the sweetbreads into small chunks and the bacon into narrow strips. Sprinkle the oysters, sweetbreads and bacon with the chopped parsley, shallots and thyme, salt and pepper.

Thread the oysters, bacon and sweetbreads alternately onto skewers. Coat with the egg, then breadcrumbs, and fry in shallow oil until golden all over.

Heat the oyster liquid with a little dry sherry and a dash of Tabasco. Arrange the skewers on a dish and serve with the liquid and crusty bread.

Trout with diced salt pork

As I sit writing at the heart of the Test Valley, it is too early yet for trout, but when they come, this is a good way to cook them. Robinson's, the very good butcher in Stockbridge, has a pickle tub and does salt belly pork, amongst other things; find yourself a good butcher near you who will do the same.

SERVES 4

100g salt belly of pork

4 trout

flour, for coating

pepper

1 glass red wine

1 lemon, quartered

Chop the pork into smallish dice and put in a heavy pan, which will eventually hold the fish. Cook gently until the pork releases its fat and turns golden. Remove and keep warm.

Gut the fish but leave the heads on. Season the flour with pepper, coat the fish and cook them in the pork fat. Don't overcook the fish: a few minutes each side will suffice. Remove the fish to plates and scatter with the lardons.

Pour the wine into the pan and allow to froth up, stirring with a wooden spoon. Pour over the fish and serve with lemon quarters.

Meat

Beef stew

What is more comforting than a good stew bubbling on the stove, smelling heavenly? You can use almost anything, but here is one that is slightly out of the ordinary. If you don't like suet dumplings, make them with butter or, best of all, chicken fat in the Jewish manner.

SERVES 4

900g stewing steak

flour, seasoned with salt, pepper, mustard powder and cayenne pepper, for coating

50g beef dripping or cooking oil

100g bacon

4 onions, roughly chopped

300ml draught cider

25g black treacle

100g celery, chopped

4 tinned anchovy fillets

sprig of thyme

75g pickled walnuts, roughly chopped

600ml beef stock

FOR THE DUMPLINGS

225g plain flour

½ teaspoon baking powder

salt and pepper

100g suet

Cut the meat into 2.5cm pieces and coat with the seasoned flour. The easiest way to do this is to put the flour into a plastic bag, add the meat and shake it all about. Heat the dripping in a sauté pan and add the coated meat cubes. Seal the meat and cook until brown, then remove to a stew pan.

Chop the bacon and cook it with the onions in the sauté pan until the onions are soft. Remove to the stew pan. Add all the other ingredients, cover and cook for 2 hours, stirring occasionally and checking liquid levels and seasoning. Alternatively, cook in the oven at 160°C/325°F/gas mark 3.

For the dumplings, sift the flour with the baking powder, a pinch of salt and a grind of pepper. Mix in the suet and enough cold water to make a stiff dough. Make the dumpling mixture into balls and add to the stew 30 minutes before the end of cooking.

Steak and kidney pudding

This is infinitely nicer than pie in my book. My recipe was given to me by Laetitia Driver, the mother of my great friend from school, Caroline. Caroline is a healer, and I probably wouldn't be walking if it wasn't for her, but her mother's Steak and Kidney Pudding is arguably more comforting. I once cooked it in a pressure cooker in my tiny kitchen at Wilde's Club and had it photographed for 'Italian Vogue'. It's wonderfully consoling.

SERVES 4

450g shin of beef

175g ox kidney

2 tablespoons flour, seasoned with salt, pepper mustard powder and cayenne pepper

1 onion, chopped

salt and pepper

4 tablespoons bitter beer

FOR THE PASTRY

225g flour

½ teaspoon salt

pinch of baking powder

110g shredded suet

150ml cold water to mix

To make the pastry, sift the flour, baking powder and salt into a bowl. Mix in the suet and enough cold water to mix to an elastic dough. Roll out the pastry to 5mm thick and line a 1.2-litre pudding basin with two-thirds of it.

Cut the beef and kidney into 2cm pieces and toss in the seasoned flour. The best way to do this is to put the meat and flour into a plastic bag and shake well. Put half of the meat into the basin then the onion, seasoning and then the rest of the meat. Pour over the beer. Use the remaining pastry to make a lid and seal well. Cover the basin with a layer of greased paper with a pleat in the middle to allow for expansion, then wrap in a cloth tied with a piece of string, secured under the basin's rim. Place in a large saucepan, pour water halfway up the basin, cover and steam for 4 hours, checking the water from time to time. If using a pressure cooker, cook for 2 hours.

Oxtail

Wonderfully delicious and comforting. Throughout the BSE scare I used to buy these, as the spinal cord of a cow doesn't extend to its tail – my friends were amazed that I could buy 'waggers' (as we used to call them when we were young).

You will notice this dish has carrots; even I, with my aversion to carrots, concede that you can't cook oxtail without them.

Cook your oxtail the day before you want to eat it. It will be better for the standing, and you will be able to skim off the excess fat. (For however hard you trim them, there always seems to be some.) One oxtail serves either three or two hungry people. When they serve it at the Cholmondeley Arms, they simply physically cannot cook enough to meet the demand.

1 oxtail

4 dessertspoons flour

cayenne pepper

salt and pepper

pinch of mustard powder

1 tablespoon oil or dripping

4 carrots, chopped

4 onions, chopped

4 sticks celery, chopped

sprig of thyme

½ bottle red wine

300ml stock

dumplings – see page 76

Trim off any surplus fat on the oxtail. Put the flour and the seasonings in a plastic bag, add the oxtail and shake until it is coated.

Heat the fat in a heavy pan and brown the oxtail. Throw in the chopped vegetables and the thyme and pour on the wine and stock. Simmer on top of the stove or in the oven at 150ºC/300ºF/gas mark 2 for hours. Remove and leave to cool overnight.

Skim the fat, then cook on top of the stove or in the oven at 160ºC/325ºF/gas mark 3 for a further 1½ hours. Add more stock, if necessary. Add the dumplings 20 minutes before the end of cooking.

Cornish pasties

I love Cornish pasties, more especially as the true pasty doesn't contain carrots; if it does, it's not Cornish, as carrots don't grow well across the Tamar. Potatoes, onions and wurzul (known as turnip) are the real ingredients. My recipe was given to me when I was a law student, by my criminal law tutor Jack Treleven, who was a Druid. Jack used margarine and lard for the pastry but I prefer to use butter and lard.

SERVES 8

900g chuck, diced small

100g potatoes, diced

100g onions, diced

100g turnips, diced

salt and pepper

FOR THE PASTRY

110g butter

110g lard

450g plain flour

salt

75ml cold water

1 egg, beaten

To make the pastry, cut up the fat and rub into the flour (to which you have added the salt), until it resembles fresh breadcrumbs. Add the water slowly and mix to a very stiff consistency. Work the mixture until it is smooth but don't overwork. Wrap in clingfilm or a plastic bag and leave to rest in a cool place for 30 minutes.

Preheat the oven to 180°C/350°F/gas mark 4.

Mix all the filling ingredients together. Roll out the pastry to 5mm thick and cut into rounds about 15cm across. Divide the filling equally between the rounds, sprinkle with a little water and draw up the edges of the pastry to meet at the top of the filling. Crimp the edges firmly together with the help of a little water and make a small slit for the steam to escape. Brush with beaten egg and bake for about 50 minutes, until golden.

Steak tartare

So-called because the Tartars or Mongol hordes were said to have ridden across the steppes with pieces of beefsteak under their saddles in order to tenderise them, this is a very reviving dish, and one which is beginning to reappear in good restaurants. Once, when we were filming for 'Clarissa and the Countryman', Johnny had terrible congestion of the lungs, verging on pleurisy. As he was due to exercise a steeplechaser on screen the next day, I intruded into the kitchens of the Cholmondeley Arms where we were staying and made him this dish. He was much improved the next day! I recently had steak tartare at Le Café Anglais; it was served with white truffles. Quite lovely.

SERVES 4

4 fillet steaks

8 anchovies, tinned

2 shallots, finely minced

Worcestershire sauce

tabasco sauce

salt and pepper

cayenne pepper

4 egg yolks

Finely chop the steaks with a sharp knife. Mix all the ingredients, except the eggs, together – adjusting the heat to the diners' choice.

Divide the mixture into four patties and place on individual plates.

Carefully place a raw egg yolk on top of each patty so that the diners can mix it in with their forks.

Hunting beef

As the title suggests, this is a dish cooked in the hunting shires. Whether for a hunt breakfast or to await your weary and wet return, it is quite delicious.

SERVES 4

900g boned and rolled brisket

900ml light ale

1 bay leaf

nutmeg

ground cloves

mixed dried herbs

Put the brisket in a pan with the ale and all the other ingredients. Bring to the boil and simmer for 2½–3 hours. Remove from the pan and leave to cool.

Salt beef

If you are lucky, your butcher will salt the meat for you; if you want to do it yourself, take a 1.8kg piece of topside or silverside and rub it all over with brown sugar, salt and about 25g saltpetre. Place in a covered bowl, turning daily for a week. The meat will keep for about 8 weeks in the salt. When you are ready to use it, soak overnight in cold water, rinse and put in a pan of fresh water.

SERVES 4

1.8kg salt silverside

175g onions, chopped

225g carrots, sliced

50g celery, chopped

100g turnips, sliced

8 cloves

100g brown sugar

½ teaspoon mustard powder

1 teaspoon ground cinnamon

juice of ½ orange

Put the meat in a large pan with the prepared vegetables. Cover with cold water and bring slowly to the boil. Remove the scum, cover and simmer gently, allowing 1 hour per 450g. Leave to cool, then remove from the liquid.

Preheat the oven to 220ºC/400ºF/gas mark 6.

Stick the cloves into the meat. Mix together the remaining ingredients and spread over the meat. Cook in the preheated oven for 45 minutes, basting from time to time. Serve hot or cold with mustard sauce.

Mollypop's hamburgers

Mollypop was the nickname my nephew, Stefan, gave my mother when she jumped out of the dining room window in fulfilment of a promise she made to get him to eat his lunch. Stefan is American and my mother was always experimenting with hamburger recipes to make him feel more at home – this was the most successful one.

SERVES 4

225g minced beef with some fat

1 x tin red peppers, finely chopped

1 tablespoon onion, finely chopped

1 teaspoon marjoram

½ teaspoon finely chopped garlic

3 tablespoons grated Cheddar

2 tablespoons milk

salt

Knead all the ingredients together with damp hands, then form into four burgers. Place under a hot grill and grill on either side until brown, or depending how cooked you like your hamburger.

Serve with your favourite relish and any other accompaniments you want.

Carpaccio of beef

Another great reviver, this dish was invented by Harry, of the Cipriani in Venice, to bring back to life guests who had overindulged in his Bellinis! If you almost freeze the meat first you will be able to cut it very thinly.

SERVES 4

500g fillet steak

good olive oil

salt and pepper

juice of 1 lemon

capers

With a sharp knife, very finely slice the beef and lay it on a dish or individual plates. Pour on a good helping of olive oil and season with salt and pepper. Pour over the lemon juice and, just before serving, decorate with the capers.

Serve with good bread and/or a rocket salad.

Shepherd's pie

There is a great deal of rubbish talked about this excellent dish. It is not a rustic invention, but part of the post-industrial nostalgia for the countryside, which was already raising its head in Victorian times, a sentimentality for a non-existent world as later manifested by green wellies and four-wheel drives among urban dwellers and an aversion to field sports.

Shepherd's pie came into the English cuisine after the Industrial Revolution, when metal grinders for mincing became available, and is designed to use up cooked lamb or mutton. The version I have given was, once again, invented by my sister Heather, who used port or whisky in the sauce. Shepherd's pie can be made beforehand and finished off before serving. It freezes well.

SERVES 6

1kg cooked lamb

3 large strong onions, chopped

lard or vegetable oil, for frying

25g butter

25g plain flour

300ml meat stock

150ml port or whisky (or use milk if preferred)

salt and freshly ground black pepper

Worcestershire sauce

FOR THE POTATO TOPPING

1kg potatoes, peeled

75g butter

a little milk

Mince the lamb. Gently fry the onions in a little fat until pale, golden and soft, then drain well.

Make a roux in a saucepan with the butter and flour and cook for 2 minutes, then slowly add the stock and other liquid to make a smooth but fairly thick sauce. Remove from the heat and mix in the meat and onions. Season well (a dash of Worcestershire sauce is a good addition) and cook over a low heat for about 3 minutes. Transfer the meat mixture to a shallow ovenproof dish and leave to cool.

Preheat the oven to 180°C/350°F/Gas 4.

For the topping, boil the potatoes in salted water until tender, then drain and leave to steam dry. Mash well with half the butter, a good amount of seasoning and a little milk (they want to be stiff).

Spread the potatoes at least 2.5cm thick over the meat, and score the top with a fork (Victorian versions say 'like a ploughed field'!). Dot the potato with the remaining butter and cook in the oven for 40 minutes. The top should be golden brown.

Lancashire hotpot

This dish is designed for the long bones of the local sheep and named for the deep brown or white pottery dish in which it was made. There are variants on the basic – in Bolton they add oysters and mushrooms, in some parts of Lancashire they add curry powder, whilst the Cumbrians add stewing beef. In Lancashire they serve it with red cabbage and add Bury black puddings to the mixture, as I have done here.

SERVES 8

8 middle-neck lamb chops (about 175g each with the bones left on)

4 lambs' kidneys, cored and sliced

25g lard or dripping

900g potatoes, sliced

salt and pepper

225g onions, sliced

2 rings of Bury black pudding

300ml stock

Preheat the oven to 180ºC/350ºF/gas mark 4.

Trim any surplus fat from the chops and fry them quickly with the kidneys (about 3–4 minutes) in the lard or dripping. Put a layer of potatoes at the bottom of a deep ovenproof dish. Lay a layer of chops and kidneys on top and season. Add some onions and black pudding and continue layering the ingredients, finishing with potatoes. Brush with melted lard or dripping. Cover and cook in the oven for 2 hours.

Remove the lid, increase the heat and place near the top of the oven. Cook for another 30 minutes to brown the potatoes.

Mutton pies

These little pies, known in Scotland as 'tuppenny struggles', are excellent travelling fare, which, with the deterioration of railway food, has become a great necessity. Despite Prince Charles' efforts to re-establish mutton, the only place you can really buy it is at a Halal butcher's (but at least it's not too hard to find one of those). Like shepherd's pie, this dish is made with cooked mutton so is handy when you have had your Sunday joint.

SERVES 4

340g hot-water crust pastry

450g cooked mutton, minced

300ml brown sauce or redcurrant jelly

salt and pepper

pinch of nutmeg

1 egg, beaten

Preheat the oven to 180ºC/350ºF/gas mark 4.

Mould the warm pastry into 6 pies, each about 9cm wide and 4cm high, saving enough for the lids. Moisten the meat with half the sauce or jelly, season and add the nutmeg. Divide the meat equally between the pie cases. Cover with pastry lids, make a hole in each and brush with egg. Bake in the preheated oven for 40 minutes.

Warm the remaining sauce or jelly and pour into the pies before serving. Eat hot or cold (but better hot).

SERVES 4

6 large potatoes

4 onions

salt and pepper

600ml stock or water

1kg scrag-end of mutton

Peel and slice the potatoes and onions.

Layer up a large saucepan with the potatoes then the mutton, seasoning as you go. Pour on the stock, cover and bring to the boil, then simmer gently for 2 hours. Check liquid levels to make sure it's not drying out. Adjust the seasoning to taste.

Irish stew

Irish stew is best made with scrag-end of mutton (and I doubt very much that the dish has anything to do with Ireland who could not have afforded the meat in Victorian times). Make this the day before so that you can skim off any excess fat. For a more lavish dish, add middle-neck chops as well.

SERVES 4

oil

2 onions, sliced

2 carrots, chopped

2 sticks celery, chopped

1 leg of mutton

salt and pepper

300ml beer

FOR THE SAUCE

50g butter

40g flour

600ml–1.2 litres boiling water

1 teaspoon lemon juice

75g capers

50ml wine or caper vinegar

In a little oil, fry the vegetables and place in a heavy flameproof casserole. Rub the joint with seasoning and place on top of the vegetables. Pour on the beer. Cook either on top of the stove at a simmer or in the oven at 160ºC/325ºF/gas mark 3, allowing 20 minutes per 450g, plus an extra 20 minutes.

To make the sauce, melt 40g butter in a pan, add the flour and work to a paste, then slowly add the boiling water, stirring as you go. When you have a sauce of the right consistency, add the lemon juice, the capers and the vinegar. Heat through. Remove from the heat and whip in the remaining 10g butter.

Boiled mutton with caper sauce

My version of this is more of a pot roast than boiled. Cooked slowly, it is a very good dish in which the full flavour of the mutton is much better, to my mind, than lamb, especially when it is taken from a wool sheep such as a Herdwick. Farmer Sharp at Borough Market has very good Herdwick mutton.

Roast pork

Everyone who eats my roast pork raves about it; the secret lies simply in the choice of pork. Without a proper covering of fat you simply can't get crackling, and most pork sold nowadays is too lean. This, I think, is why no one is eating it and why the pig farmers are going out of business. If you don't have a butcher to score the meat, use a Stanley knife. The other tip comes from Fanny Craddock, who said to rub the salt and oil into the rind as if into the face of your worst enemy. (Blair is still good or even Brown, but you can pick your own.)

SERVES 4

olive oil

sea salt

1.8kg loin or leg of pork, scored for crackling

Preheat the oven to 220°C/425°F/gas mark 7.

Rub a little oil and then the salt into the crackling. Roast in the preheated oven for 30 minutes, then reduce the heat to 160°C/325°F/gas mark 3, allowing 20 minutes per 450g in total.

Savoy pork chops

This dish was a favourite at the Savoy grill. I used to love the old Savoy grill, as did everyone else. My mother once saw the great opera singer Chaliapin whisk Nellie Melba off her feet there and swing her around as if she were a small child. Sadly, the place was ruined and now it seems to be gone forever. Bas à Celebrity Chefs.

SERVES 4

50g butter

8 thick pork chops

225g cooking apples, peeled and diced

100g sultanas

2 teaspoons grated lemon zest

salt and pepper

300ml stock

150ml medium sherry

Melt the butter in a large sauté pan and quickly brown the chops on both sides. Add the apples, sultanas and lemon zest, season and pour over the stock and the sherry. Cover and simmer gently for 1–1½ hours.

Remove the chops to a serving dish, reduce the sauce (thickening with flour or cornflour if you like) and pour over the chops.

Zampone
WITH WHITE POLENTA AND CREMONA MUSTARD

This is a dish I ate one Sunday at my beloved Valvona and Crolla. Now, you may if you wish cook, bone and stuff your pigs' trotters, and I will be the first to encourage you; however, the Italians produce a very good stuffed trotter or zampone, which takes all the hassle out of this dish. Simply prepare it according to the instructions on the packet. Polenta is maize flour and therefore suitable for those with a wheat allergy. If you can't get white polenta, use yellow; the white is made from a different type of maize and has a more delicate flavour and Italians who still care about seasonal treats serve it around Christmas. Some people are nervous of cooking polenta, but as is so often the case in cooking, it is all in the wrist action.

Mostarda di Cremona is that strange Italian mustard made with what looks like glacé fruits in a mustard liquid – you can buy it in any Italian deli.

SERVES 4

1 zampone

350g polenta

salt and pepper

1 jar mostarda di Cremona

Cook the zampone according to the instructions.

Bring a pot of lightly salted water to the boil and stir in the polenta. Stir continuously to avoid lumps and cook until you have a smooth porridge. Season.

On a warmed serving dish, spread your polenta as a base, then slice the zampone and arrange on top. Slice the fruit from the mustard and arrange like jewels around the zampone.

Sausage casserole

Such a cheap and comforting dish for an evening by the fire or kitchen supper with friends. Much is down to the quality of the sausages, but that's not a problem nowadays with so many butchers making good ones. As someone who has judged the great Yorkshire Pork Pie and Sausage competition three times, I know quite a lot about them! Choose ones whose skins are well filled (but not overfilled or they will burst).

SERVES 4

900g sausages

4 onions, sliced

oil

1 garlic clove, chopped

salt and pepper

1 x 400g tin tomatoes

bottle of beer or ½ bottle red wine

Preheat the oven to 180ºC/350ºF/gas mark 4.

In a heavy flameproof casserole, brown the sausages and set aside. Then fry the onions in a little oil until coloured. Add the garlic and cook a little longer. Arrange the sausages on top, season, pour on the tomatoes and the alcohol and cook gently in the preheated oven for about 1 hour.

Serve with lots of mash, flavoured with cheese or horseradish or mustard.

Loin of veal with its own kidneys

This is a dish my sister Heather used to make, and very good it is too. Get your butcher to bone a piece of veal loin and stuff it with its own kidneys, preferably with some of their fat casing left on.

SERVES 4

50g lard

1.8kg veal loin with its own kidneys

3 onions, sliced

salt and pepper

1 bottle red wine

Preheat the oven to 230ºC/450ºF/gas mark 8.

Heat the lard in a large pan and brown your veal joint all over. Remove the joint from the pan and fry the onions until coloured. Transfer the onions to a deep roasting pan or casserole and place the joint on top. Season well and pour on the red wine.

Cook in the preheated oven for 20 minutes, then reduce the heat to 160ºC/325ºF/gas mark 3. Allow 20 minutes per 450g, plus an extra 20 minutes.

SERVES 4

1.3kg boned breast of veal

22 stuffed olives

1 teaspoon caraway seeds

1 teaspoon lemon juice

6 anchovy fillets

1 garlic clove, finely chopped

1 tablespoon flour

black pepper

bacon fat

Preheat the oven to 220ºC/425ºF/gas mark 7.

Wash and dry the veal breast. Cut the olives in half and lay on the meat. Sprinkle with the caraway seeds and lemon juice and then lay on the anchovies. Roll up the veal and stitch up the ends.

Mix the garlic, flour and black pepper and rub on the outside of the meat, then smear with the bacon fat. Roast in the preheated oven for 10 minutes, then reduce the heat to 180ºC/350ºF/gas mark 4 and cook for about another 1½ hours.

Serve hot or cold.

Veal with olive and anchovy

This is a dish my mother loved to make. People avoid veal or lamb breasts because they think they are difficult to cook. They're not and they have the advantage of being cheap —good in these credit crunch days.

Poultry & game

Chicken curry

A really simple chicken curry for those days when you know better than to order a take-away. Serve with rice, poppadoms and any Indian side dishes of your choice (I've used a cucumber raita and tomato and onion salad here).

SERVES 4

2 tablespoons fat (if there is fat on chicken, render it down; if not, use ghee)

1 chicken, approx. 1.8kg, jointed from its carcass

2 onions, chopped

2 garlic cloves, chopped

2 red chillies, chopped

1 teaspoon each fenugreek seeds and garam masala (alternatively, use 2 teaspoons curry powder)

1 teaspoon dried mint

1 teaspoon coriander seeds, lightly pounded

6 green or black cardamom pods

1 teaspoon turmeric

small piece of tamarind

1 pickled lemon, chopped (optional)

600ml stock from the carcass

Heat the fat, brown the chicken joints and transfer to a cooking pot. Fry the onions, garlic and chillies in the remaining fat. Add all the spices (including cardamom pods, turmeric and tamarind) and allow the onions to soften. Stir, so the spices are well mixed in. Add the spice mixture to the pot with the chicken, along with the pickled lemon, if using. Pour on the stock, stir well and bring to the boil. Cover and simmer gently for about 1 hour or until the chicken is cooked. Uncover for the last 10 minutes of cooking, so that the sauce reduces slightly. You may want to remove the cardamom pods before serving.

Chicken with whole spices

This is a very simple Bengali chicken dish, very slowly cooked. Kashmiri chillies aren't particularly hot and are more like dried paprika, which can be used instead. It's an interesting-looking dish and is good for a supper party.

SERVES 4

1 medium chicken, cut in pieces

5 medium onions, finely sliced

50g ghee

3 Kashmiri chillies

4 bay leaves

10 cloves

12 crushed peppercorns

thumb-sized piece of root ginger, thinly sliced

2 garlic cloves, finely sliced

300ml yogurt

salt to taste

pinch of saffron

Mix all the ingredients in a flameproof casserole and marinate for 30 minutes, turning from time to time. Cover tightly, using foil to reinforce the seal, and cook very slowly on a low heat for 2 hours. Check the chicken and cook for a further 30 minutes. You can also cook this in a slow oven at 130°C/275°F/gas mark 1.

Soak the saffron in a little warm milk. Add to the dish and cook for a few minutes longer. Serve with rice.

Chicken and salsify pie

My friend Douglas raised salsify (or oyster plant, as it is also known); I love the flavour and it's particularly good with chicken, so this is a comforting pie.

SERVES 4

900g salsify

lemon juice

50g butter

1 onion, chopped

2 garlic cloves, crushed

1 chicken, jointed and skinned

1 bouquet garni

150ml dry white wine

salt and pepper

100g flour

225ml double cream

2 tablespoons parsley, chopped

2 egg yolks

juice of 1 lemon

450–700g shortcrust pastry (depending on the size of the pie dish)

Peel the salsify and place in a bowl. Pour in a little water with lemon juice to prevent discolouring.

Melt 25g butter in a large pan and cook the onions and the garlic until soft. Remove them and add the chicken pieces to seal them. Add the salsify (drained), the bouquet garni, the wine and enough water to cover, if necessary. Season and simmer for 30–40 minutes or until the salsify is cooked. Strain, setting aside the stock, and throw out the bouquet garni.

Cut the salsify into manageable pieces and strip the chicken from the bones.

Make a roux with the remaining butter and the flour and add enough of the stock to make a thick béchamel sauce. Add the cream and parsley, season and return the chicken and salsify to the sauce. Cook gently for another 5 minutes. Remove from the heat. Beat the egg yolks with the lemon juice and stir into the mixture. Allow everything to cool and completely thicken.

Preheat the oven to 230ºC/450ºF/gas mark 8.

Line your pie dish with pastry, leaving an overlap. Spoon in the chicken mixture and place a support for the lid in the centre. Cover with the remaining pastry, seal the edges well and glaze with milk or egg, making a small hole for the steam to escape.

Bake in the preheated oven for 20 minutes, then reduce the heat to 190ºC/375ºF/gas mark 5 for a further 30 minutes, or until the pastry is golden.

Devilled chicken with breadcrumbs

This is a dish my mother used to make once my father had left, and we no longer had servants. My mother only knew about five dishes, having never cooked, and this was one of them. I loved it then and I do now.

SERVES 4

225g butter

1 chicken, jointed and skinned

2 teaspoons Worcestershire sauce

2 teaspoons Tabasco sauce

2 teaspoons cayenne pepper

1½ teaspoons dry mustard

salt

juice of 1 lemon

100g large fresh white breadcrumbs

Preheat the oven to 160°C/325°F/gas mark 3.

Heat half the butter in a pan and brown the chicken pieces. Transfer to an ovenproof dish. Mix together all the remaining ingredients, except the breadcrumbs and remaining butter, and pour over the chicken. Lay the breadcrumbs on top and dot with the remaining butter. Cook uncovered in the preheated oven for about 50 minutes to 1 hour, or until the chicken is cooked.

Guinea fowl

I find guinea fowl more exotic than pheasant or peacock, with its strange cave-drawing shape, designer plumage and weird cry, like a creaking gate. Its eggs are like a practical joke – hard as china; and at a full moon they will keep you awake all night.

SERVES 4

50g celery, chopped

5 sprigs watercress, chopped

salt and pepper

225g butter

2 lemons

2 guinea fowl, 700g each

2 garlic cloves, crushed

100g pork fat or bacon

150ml dry white wine

600ml stock

4 egg yolks

Mix the celery and watercress together in a bowl, season and bind with 50g melted butter. Grate the rind of the lemons and mix with some salt and pepper, then rub the skin of the birds with the lemon mixture. Put any remaining lemon mixture and the garlic inside the birds. Tie the pork fat or bacon over the birds with some string.

Heat 100g butter in a pan and brown the birds all over. Remove the birds from the pan and pour in the wine. Reduce slightly, then add the stock.

Stuff the birds with the watercress and celery mixture but don't truss them. Return the birds to the pan, cover, and simmer for 45 minutes. Remove the guinea fowl and carve them onto a hot dish.

Squeeze the lemons and beat their juice with the egg yolks. Add a little hot stock, stir well and pour into the pan. Blend in the remaining butter and allow the sauce to thicken. Do not let it boil. Pour over the carved birds and serve, garnished with watercress and celery leaves.

Duck fritters

This is a great way to use up a leftover duck. I often order roast duck in a Chinese restaurant and take home a doggy bag of the leftovers! These are quite delicious and make a great starter or supper dish.

½ roast duck

4 eggs

450g cooked rice

4 spring onions, finely sliced

½ teaspoon five-spice powder

dash of soy sauce

2 teaspoons hoi sin sauce

⅔ vegetable oil to ⅓ sesame oil, for frying

Cut the duck meat into small pieces. Break the eggs into a bowl and beat. Add the duck pieces, rice, spring onions, five-spice powder, soy sauce and hoi sin. Heat the oil in a heavy pan, drop spoonfuls of the mixture into the pan and fry until golden on each side.

PICKLE:

2 aubergines

125ml oil

2 tomatoes, chopped

1 small red chilli, chopped

1 pickled lemon, sliced

4 tablespoons rice or white wine vinegar

2 tablespoons caster sugar

To make the pickle, slice the aubergine and fry in the oil until soft. Add the tomatoes, the chilli and the lemon and fry gently for 5 minutes. Add the other ingredients and continue to cook until it all comes together. Chop the pickle, once cooled.

Serve the fritters with the pickle.

Teal

COOKED WITH RED WINE, WITH AN ORANGE AND ONION SALAD

This is a variant on the delicious dish I ate at Rowley Leigh's splendid new restaurant Le Café Anglais. Teal, the smallest of our native wild ducks, is quite delicious. I remember the night before Johnny and I flew to New York for 'UK with NY' post 9/11, we treated ourselves to dinner at the Connaught in the days when it had the best belle époque restaurant left in Europe. We had teal, flambéed in Armagnac at our table. I was so sad when it was Ramsay-fied that I never went there again, even though I admire Angela Hartnett, the chef he installed there. If you can't get teal, any wild duck breast will do, but adjust the cooking time according to size.

SERVES 4

1 tablespoon olive oil

4 teal breasts

250ml bottle red wine

1 dessertspoon brandy

2 onions, thinly sliced

1 small head fennel, thinly sliced

2 oranges, peeled (pith removed) and sliced

25g small olives

salt and pepper

In a sauté pan, heat the oil and brown and season the meat. Pour in the red wine, cover and simmer gently for about 10 minutes – they should be very pink. Remove the lid, pour on the brandy, ignite and allow to burn off.

On each hot plate, layer the thinly sliced onions, fennel and oranges. Lay on the breasts and scatter over the olives.

Pour over the pan juices and eat with gusto.

Duck with turnips

This is a classic French country dish that makes a very cosy dish for a cold spring evening. Why spring? Young turnips, eaten seasonally. I use Aylesbury or another domestic duck, not a wild one.

SERVES 4

1 duck

salt and pepper

3 tablespoons duck fat

100g streaky bacon, diced

2 onions, sliced

150ml dry white wine

125ml stock

24 button onions, peeled

450g small turnips, peeled

pinch of sugar

1 tablespoon flour

1 glass of Madeira

Season the duck. Heat half the duck fat in a pan and brown the bird all over. Transfer to a large flameproof casserole and fry the bacon and onions in the casserole. Add the wine and stock, cover and cook gently for 1 hour.

Brown the button onions and the turnips in the remaining fat. When they begin to brown, add some juices from the duck, cook gently and, when the liquid is almost gone, add a good pinch of sugar to glaze. Transfer the duck to a dish and keep warm.

Strain the casserole liquid into a clean pan, remove any excess fat and reduce if necessary. Mix the flour with the Madeira and stir into the sauce.

Arrange the vegetables around the duck and serve the sauce separately.

Cretan rabbit pie

I'm not really sure that there are many rabbits on Crete, but this is an adaptation of one of their chicken dishes, which works really well with rabbit. You can either cut the flesh off the bones before cooking or, for greater ease, cut it into pieces. This dish can also be made and served as individual pies.

SERVES 4

2 tablespoons olive oil

2 good-size rabbits

2 tablespoons seasoned flour

juice of 1 lemon

cayenne pepper

2 onions, roughly chopped

1 garlic clove, chopped

knob of butter

175g cooked rice

1 tablespoon sultanas

1 tablespoon capers, halved

225g Cheshire cheese, cubed and sliced

white stock to moisten

salt and pepper

1 packet puff pastry

Preheat the oven to 200°C/400°F/gas 6.

Heat the oil in a pan. Toss the meat in the seasoned flour and brown in the oil. Remove the meat, pour over the lemon juice, sprinkle with cayenne pepper and set aside.

Fry the onion and garlic in the butter, until soft. Mix with the rice and put into a buttered pie dish. Arrange the meat on top, then the sultanas and capers. Sprinkle over a few cubes of cheese. Pour in any remaining lemon juice from the marinade and any stock you think necessary. Season lightly. Arrange a layer of sliced cheese over the mixture.

Roll out the pastry and cover the pie. Bake in the preheated oven for 40 minutes, until the pastry is risen and golden.

Partridge with truffled sausages

In good Italian and French delis you can buy little jars of truffled sausages. They aren't cheap but a little goes a very long way and gosh, are they good and comforting. They go well with eggs but they also taste good with partridge. I love partridge, especially the English native grey-leg; for red-legs you have to try a little harder and this dish does very well.

SERVES 4

100g butter

4 partridges

2 onions, finely chopped

100g pearl barley

1.2 litres salted water

3 truffled sausages

salt and pepper

approx. 125ml white stock

Preheat the oven to 180°C/350°F/gas mark 4.

In an ovenproof sauté pan, melt half the butter and brown the partridges all over. Remove the birds and fry the onions. Boil the barley in the salted water for about 45 minutes, or until cooked but not too soft. Cut two of the sausages into pieces and place inside the partridges. Mix the onions with the barley, then add the remaining sausage, cut into small pieces. Season well.

Bed the partridges into the barley base, pour over a little of the oil from the sausage jar and the white stock. Cover and roast in the preheated oven for 40 minutes and uncover for the last 10 minutes.

Pheasant with dates and walnuts

This is a dish I invented for a Countryside Alliance demonstration (cooking not barricades!) in Hampshire. The pheasant is a Circassian bird brought to us by the Romans. Its birthplace is more allied to the dates, walnuts and pomegranates of Persia, so I hope you like this.

SERVES 4

2–3 tablespoons olive oil

1 pheasant, jointed and skinned

175g walnuts

2 garlic cloves

2 sticks of celery, chopped

150ml white wine

1 tablespoon juice

75g chopped dates

175g pomegranate seeds

leaves removed from a small bunch of parsley

Preheat the oven to 160ºC/325ºF/gas mark 3.

In a heavy ovenproof pan, heat 1 tablespoon olive oil and use to brown the pheasant pieces.

In a food processor, chop the walnuts into small pieces, add the garlic and work some more – you can do all this with a pestle and mortar. Transfer to a bowl, add the celery and pour on the remaining olive oil to create an emulsified paste.

Remove the pheasant pieces from the pan and stir the paste into the oil. Cook gently for a few minutes, then stir in the wine and pomegranate juice. Add the chopped dates, return the pheasant pieces to the pan and cook in the preheated oven for 30–40 minutes. Stir in the pomegranate seeds and the parsley 10 minutes before the end.

Venison schnitzel

My friend Isabel says venison must be cooked either very slowly or very quickly. This dish falls into the latter category. I sometimes add stewed plums to the sauce or, even better, the pickled umeboshi plums from Japan. Alternatively, you can now buy umeboshi paste, and a teaspoon or two stirred into the sauce instead of the vinegar is very good.

If the piece of venison is in any way tough, marinate it overnight in olive oil or red wine, and then dry it carefully.

SERVES 4

1 slice venison per person, beaten thin between sheets of clingfilm

seasoned flour

butter and olive oil

capers

salt and pepper

1 wine glass port

1 teaspoon sherry vinegar

hard-boiled eggs, chopped

Flour the venison slices. Heat the oil and butter together in a heavy frying pan and flash-fry the meat. Throw in the capers and fry for a moment. Transfer the meat and capers to a warmed plate. Pour the port into the pan to deglaze it, bring to the boil and pour in the sherry vinegar. Pour this over the meat.

Garnish with hard-boiled eggs and serve with fried potatoes.

Vegetables

Pommes clarise

This simple method of cooking potatoes was so dubbed by my nephew Edward. It is the simplest of gratins and you can use anything that takes your fancy. In this dish, I have added two large sliced tomatoes and two sprigs of thyme. A great dish with a roast.

SERVES 4–6

1kg potatoes

125g butter

salt and freshly ground black pepper

freshly grated nutmeg

650ml double cream

Peel and slice your potatoes to the thickness of a 10-pence piece. Wash well in several changes of cold water to remove the starch, then pat dry.

Butter an ovenproof dish and put in a layer of potatoes. Season with salt, pepper and nutmeg, and dot with butter. Continue to add layers of potatoes, seasoning and butter until the dish is half full, then pour on half the cream.

Continue the process and then pour over the rest of the cream. Put into a medium oven under the roast and cook for 1–1½hours, depending on the heat of the oven. (That is, if the roast is at 160°C/325°F/Gas 3, give the potatoes 1½ hours; if at 180–190°C/350–375°F/Gas 4–5, 1 hour.)

Gratin of ham and chicory rolls

This combination of ham with cheese and chicory is one of my favourites. It is total comfort food to me and, living alone, I get the dish to scrape…

SERVES 6

6 slices of cooked ham

6 chicory heads

salt

600ml white sauce

175g strong Cheddar cheese, grated

1 teaspoon English mustard powder

1 teaspoon cayenne pepper

butter, for greasing

Preheat the oven to 200°C/400°F/Gas 6.

Remove the cores of the chicory. Put the chicory into salted boiling water and cook for 5 minutes. Drain well.

Heat the white sauce and melt two-thirds of the cheese into it. Stir in the mustard powder and cayenne.

Carefully wrap the ham slices around the chicory, and place in a buttered ovenproof dish. Pour over the sauce, scatter on the rest of the cheese, and bake in the oven for 30 minutes, until the sauce is bubbling and the top golden.

Stuffed cardoons

As you may know, I owe it all to the cardoon, which gave me my television debut with Pat Llewellyn on Sophie Grigson's 'Eat your Greens'. This recipe was the first dish I ever cooked on TV and I love it still.

SERVES 4

2–3 cardoon stalks

FOR THE STUFFING

450g minced lamb

2 shallots, very finely chopped

2 garlic cloves, very finely chopped

½ teaspoon ground cumin

½ teaspoon chilli powder

½ teaspoon ground coriander

salt and pepper

1 egg, beaten

2 tablespoons flour

2 tablespoons olive oil

Preheat the oven to 180ºC/350ºF/gas mark 4.

Cut the cardoon stalks into 5cm lengths. Blanche them in boiling acidulated water for about 5 minutes. Drain and refresh under a cold tap, then dry on a cloth.

To make the stuffing, mix all the ingredients together and leave to stand for 1 hour or more.

Take a piece of cardoon stalk and stuff it with the lamb mixture, then sandwich together using another piece of stalk. Repeat until all the stalks are stuffed. Dip in the egg, then the flour.

Heat the olive oil in a heavy sauté pan and fry each of the sandwiches until they are browned all over. Transfer to a buttered oven dish and cook in the preheated oven for about 30 minutes.

Simply serve with a sauce made with tinned chopped tomatoes heated through with some cumin, coriander and chilli.

Pease pudding

What does the rhyme say? 'Pease pudding hot, pease pudding cold, pease pudding in the pot, nine days old.' Oh, I love pease pudding. In Durham it is still sold commercially and spread on 'stottie bread' (bread cooked in the bottom of the oven) or good ham with the fat on. Whenever I cook a ham or a piece of pickled pork, I add a clothful of peas to cook with it. I also freeze my ham stock so I can cook peas in it at a later date.

SERVES 6–8

1kg split peas

ham stock

2 egg yolks

25g butter

salt and freshly ground black pepper

Soak the peas overnight in plenty of cold water. Tie the soaked and drained peas loosely in a cloth and boil in plenty of ham stock to cover (or with a ham) for about 1½ hours.

Remove from the pan and untie, then rub the peas through a sieve or mouli. Dry the peas in a pan over a gentle heat until thick, then stir in the butter, egg yolks and salt and pepper to taste.

Puntarella with bagna calda

Puntarella is one of those strange looking, slightly bitter vegetables beloved of Italians (and me). A member of the chicory family, it appears in Italian delis around Christmas and into the spring. It's one of those vegetables which, in ancient times, kept scurvy away during the winter months. It has a rounded stem made up of small stalks with green, pointy leaves which, my friend Mary Contini at Valvonna and Crolla where I buy it tells me, are very good for wrapping around fish as you cook them. (Rather, I suppose, as they do in the Philippines with cardoon leaves.) I must confess, I have never tried it, but have no reason to doubt her. If you don't want your puntarella on toast, serve it in a bowl with the sauce mixed in. If you don't have any puntarella, use some other chicory-type vegetable.

SERVES 4

1 puntarella

4 garlic cloves

6 tinned anchovy fillets

olive oil

sourdough or rustic bread

Cut the leaves and the root end from the puntarella and slice the stalks into 3–5cm pieces. Put these into very cold water for about an hour. Drain and dry in a cloth. With a pestle and mortar, pound the garlic cloves and anchovy fillets to a paste. Slowly pour in the olive oil, stirring as you go, until you have a thick, emulsified sauce.

Cut the bread and toast the slices, transfer to a plate and lay the puntarella on top. Pour on the sauce and serve.

Greens

This way of cooking greens will do well for any strong greens: spring cabbage, pak choy, broccoli and so on. The trick is not to cook them with much water. The addition of anchovies or dried shrimp is my friend Karen's and makes it more interesting.

2 heads of spring cabbage or the equivalent

100g butter or 2 tablespoons olive oil

1 small onion, finely chopped

1 clove garlic, finely chopped

1 small chilli, finely chopped (optional)

salt and pepper

small tin of anchovies in oil, cut in half or 1 tablespoon dried shrimps

Wash the greens and lightly shake: the water remaining on the leaves should be enough for cooking. Shred the cabbage. Melt the butter or the oil in a heavy pan. Fry the onion, garlic and chilli for a few minutes, then add the greens, turning well. Season, cover and cook until done, about 12–15 minutes, stirring occasionally. Stir in the anchovies or dried prawns. It's even better reheated.

25g flour

25g butter

600ml milk

1 teaspoon mustard powder

salt and pepper

100g mature Cheddar

1 cauliflower

25g grated Cheddar or parmesan

Cauliflower cheese

Again an ultimate comfort dish: what can be more comforting than this cheap simple dish? I believe that people buy it ready made in supermarkets – sometimes I really do despair of the human race – but freshly made, with a good-quality cauliflower, and there is nothing more enjoyable and easy.

Make a white sauce with the flour, butter and milk. Stir in the mustard powder, season, then add the 100g cheese; stir until it melts.

Preheat the oven to 180ºC/350ºF/gas mark 4.

Wash your cauliflower and drain. Cut off the root end and trim of most off the leaves; I like to leave some green on to hold the cauli together. Cook the cauli in a pan of boiling salted water to which you have added a bay leaf to stop the horrid smell (don't remove the bay leaf until you drain the vegetable). When the cauli is just cooked, drain and put it in a deep dish and pour over the sauce.

Sprinkle on the grated cheese and cook in the oven until the sauce on the top is browning nicely. Serve with cold meat or bacon.

Puddings & baking

Pears and Oranges

When I was growing up, we had a number of wild pear trees in the garden – very old and left over from when St John's Wood was a real wood, or maybe from the garden of the monastery that gave the area its name. We were forever looking for ways to use them as they were definitely not eaters. This curious cold pudding – which I think must have been my mother's invention – turned out to be a good way of serving them. Great for hot days or cold buffets.

SERVES 4

900g cooking pears, peeled, cored and quartered

135g sugar

4 large oranges

Poach the pears in a syrup made from 75g sugar and 300ml water, until cooked. Transfer them to a serving dish.

Thinly peel the rind from 2 of the oranges and cut into thin strips. Cook in a little water until tender, then strain and set aside. Peel the remaining oranges, removing all the pith, and divide into segments. Add to the pears, then chill in the fridge.

Boil the remaining 50g sugar with 1 tablespoon water to make caramel. Allow the caramel to set on an oiled plate and crush into small pieces. Scatter over the dish of fruit and decorate with the orange peel. Serve with cream.

Buttered oranges

This is a 17th century dish from the pastry cook Anne Blencowe. Sweet oranges first came to Britain at this time from Ceylon and were a luxury. It is wonderful to see these filled oranges being brought to the table in a basket lined with a napkin and the surprised rapture when the diners discover the filling. Removing all the pith from the orange shells takes some effort, but it is worth it – and every time I have served them to knowledgeable foodies they have gone mad for them.

SERVES 4

6 oranges or tangerines (for filling), plus 2 large oranges

5 egg yolks, lightly beaten

50g caster sugar

1 teaspoon rose water

100g unsalted butter

300ml double cream

1 large piece soft candied orange peel

Carefully empty out your oranges or tangerines for the shells, keeping a lid for each. Take care to remove all the pith, but be careful not to break the skin.

Grate the rind from the 2 extra oranges and then squeeze the juice. In the top of a double boiler mix together the orange juice and rind, the egg yolks and sugar. Stir gently, scraping down the sides from time to time. When the mixture starts to ribbon, remove from the top of the pan and stand in a basin of cold water to cool slightly. Continue to stir and add the rose water. Remove from the cold water.

Cut the butter into 5cm cubes and whisk into the mixture one by one, incorporating each before moving on to the next. Half whip the cream and fold into the mixture. As the mixture starts to set, cut the candied peel into tiny pieces and stir in so that they are suspended rather than sinking to the bottom.

Fill each orange shell and replace the lid. Cool thoroughly so the mixture is set, before you serve.

Quinces

The Millisons, who live in my village, have a quince tree and in a good year I am given some. The aroma of quinces which then pervades my house is both comforting and seductive. Poached and bottled, they are a glowing pink to delight the larder; baked in the oven and then scraped from the skin, beaten with brown sugar and served with cream, they are comforting indeed. But for me they work perhaps best of all in this dish with raisins.

As I no longer take alcohol, I substitute orange juice mixed with balsamic vinegar for the sherry.

SERVES 4

900g quinces, peeled, cored and sliced

100g butter

225g stoned raisins

100g sugar

300ml Amontillado sherry

Simmer the quinces in melted butter until soft. Add the raisins, sugar and sherry and cook gently until the sugar has dissolved.

Serve warm or cold with cream.

Gooseberry fool

Any kind of fruit can be made into a fool, but I like the gooseberry version best. If you sift the cooked fruit rather than liquidise it, you will avoid the abrasive, hairy quality that people complain about.

SERVES 4

900g gooseberries

2 sprigs elderflower

175g sugar

2 tablespoons orange flower water

300ml double cream

3 egg yolks

300ml milk

40g caster sugar

Top and tail the gooseberries, simmer them in 30ml water with the elderflower until soft, and sweeten to taste. Remove the elderflower sprigs, add the orange flower water, then pass the fruit through a fine sieve. Leave to cool.

Whip the cream lightly. Make a custard with the eggs, milk and caster sugar and leave to cool. Mix the fruit pulp with the custard and fold in the cream. Pour into individual dishes or a large, decorative bowl and chill in the fridge before serving.

Apple jalousie

This incredibly easy emergency pudding is named after the French word for 'blinds' because of the way the pastry is cut. Apples and marmalade are something readily found in my house and I usually have a packet of puff pastry in the freezer; otherwise you can knock up some shortcrust or rough puff quickly. I only ever make puff pastry if I am treating myself to croissants.

I use tart eating apples for this pudding, as I like the apple to keep its texture rather than collapse.

SERVES 4

225g puff pastry

175g marmalade

450g apples, peeled, cored and sliced

egg or milk to glaze

caster sugar for dredging

Preheat the oven to 220°C/425°F/gas mark 7.

Roll out the pastry to a 30cm and cut in half. Place one half on a lightly greased baking sheet. Roll out the other half to 32 x 20cm and fold in half lengthways. With a sharp knife, cut into the folded edge at 1cm intervals to within 2.5cm of the ends.

Spread marmalade over the pastry on the baking sheet, leaving a 2.5cm margin around the edges, then cover the marmalade with the sliced apples. Brush the edges with egg or milk. Unfold the sliced pastry carefully and place on top knocking up the edges with a knife.

Brush the top with egg or milk and dredge evenly with sugar.

Bake in the preheated oven for 25–30 minutes or until golden brown. Serve hot or cold, preferably with cream.

Rice pudding

Shades of childhood and, for me, the perfect comfort food. When I go and visit my friend April O'Leary who taught me at school, I always pester her for rice pudding (which she makes very well on top of the stove, so no skin; I quite like skin, however, so I make mine in the oven). Over the years I have collected many rice pudding recipes, including the rather grand Marquis Pudding (opposite), so I offer some of these variations for your delectation.

SERVES 4

75g short-grain rice

50g caster sugar

pinch of salt

small dash of vanilla

essence

1.2 litres full-fat milk

grind of nutmeg

25g butter

Preheat the oven to 150ºC/300ºF/gas mark 2.

Wash the rice and put it in a 1.8-litre pie dish with the sugar, salt and vanilla. Stir in the milk, grate on the nutmeg and dot with butter. Bake in the preheated oven until the rice is cooked, stirring in the skin twice during baking.

Variations

For the boiled version: bring the milk to the boil and stir in the rice and other ingredients. Simmer for 1 hour.

For *pwdin reis mamgu* (the Welsh version): leave out the sugar but add a bay leaf. Cook as for boiled, then remove the bay leaf and cool slightly. Mix in 4 egg yolks, stiffly beat the 4 egg whites and fold into the pudding. Bake at 220ºC/245ºF/gas mark 7 for 10–15 minutes until the top has browned on. Serve with jam, honey or fruit.

Marquis pudding

I don't know who the marquis may have been but he had good taste. This is a pudding we used to eat at home, slightly unusual and very enjoyable.

SERVES 4

600ml milk

40g short-grain rice

100g caster sugar

150ml double cream

100g apricot jam

450g stewed cooking apples

75g ground almonds

1 egg

Preheat the oven to 180°C/350°F/gas mark 4.

Bring the milk to the boil, scatter in the rice and simmer. After 40 minutes, stir in 25g sugar and continue cooking until the rice is done. Leave to cool slightly.

Half whip the cream and fold into the rice. Spread a layer of jam at the bottom of a deep pie dish, then add a layer of stewed apples and a layer of rice. Repeat until the dish is two-thirds full. Mix the remaining sugar with the ground almonds and the egg and spoon in small peaks over the top. Bake in the preheated oven for 35 minutes.

This can be served with melted apricot jam flavoured with brandy.

Caramelised pineapple crumble

Everyone loves crumble. However, nowadays you seem to find that in the interests of trying to be different crumble toppings are mixed with nuts or muesli or oats, all of which are anathema to me. I like my crumble topping made with flour, butter and sugar, and that's it. When I was in the West Indies we ate lots of pineapple, largely because it was ripened in situ, sweet as manna and delicious. The fruit you buy over here is, quite frankly, disappointing, but I hope I have found a way round this by caramelising it. On its own, I find the pineapple overpowering, but it is good either mixed with apple or banana (the latter in this country is rather on a par with the pineapples, but in this instance that is an advantage).

1 small pineapple

25g butter

110g light brown sugar

6 bananas, sliced

225g plain flour

110g unsalted butter, plus extra to dot on top

75g caster sugar

Preheat the oven to 190ºC/375ºF/gas mark 5.

Cut the peel from the pineapple and cut the flesh into pieces, removing the core.

Melt the butter in a heavy frying pan. Add the brown sugar and a little water and boil to form a syrup. Add the pineapple pieces and turn them until they are sticky and caramelised. Transfer to an ovenproof dish, layering with the sliced bananas. Pour over any remaining syrup.

Sift the flour into a bowl, cut the butter into pieces and mix with the flour to form the consistency of crumbs. Stir in the sugar.

Spread the crumble mixture over the top of the pineapple and banana mixture and dot with butter. Place in the preheated oven and bake for about 45 minutes, until the top is golden and the filling bubbling.

Serve with lots of custard and/or double cream.

Cornish junket

Junket – you either love it or you hate it, and it is probably not much known to today's younger generation. I love it, and urge you to try it before you condemn it. Junket is set with rennet, which comes from the lining of a calf's stomach (so not suitable for vegetarians). The Cornish version has added clotted cream.

The trick with junket is to warm the milk only to blood heat (also known as curds and cream, summoning up visions of Little Miss Muffet). And you can add any flavour you like: fruit syrup, cocoa or brandy. The measurement I give is for pasteurised milk, but you should halve this if you are lucky enough to have real milk.

SERVES 4

600ml milk

1 tablespoon sugar

3–4 sugar lumps rubbed on the cut side of a lemon

1 tablespoon flavouring (optional)

1 tablespoon rennet

1 pot of clotted cream

Warm the milk to blood heat, add the sugar, then the sugar lumps. Transfer to a serving dish and stir in the rennet and any flavouring. Leave to stand for around 30 minutes at room temperature until set. Cover with clotted cream, chill in the fridge and serve.

Marmalade batter pudding

My Aberdonian grandmother loved this pudding. (Scotland is, as you probably know, the home of marmalade as we know it.) This recipe is also a very good way of using any marmalade that has gone a bit crusty. It is a very simple, quick and scrummy pudding.

SERVES 6–10

350g plain flour

pinch of salt

100g sugar

1 teaspoon ground ginger

grated rind of 1 lemon and 1 orange

600ml milk

8 eggs, separated

175g orange marmalade

Preheat the oven to 200°C/400°F/gas mark 6.

Sift the flour and mix with the salt, sugar, ginger and lemon and orange rind. Mix to a batter with the milk and the egg yolks. Stiffly beat the egg whites and fold into the mixture.

Grease and line a basin or baking tin and spread with the marmalade. Pour in the batter and bake in the preheated oven for 20 minutes.

Turn the pudding out onto a plate. Serve with a marmalade sauce, made with melted marmalade, the juice of the lemon and orange used above and, if you fancy, a dash of whisky or Grand Marnier.

Bread and butter pudding

This is very popular nowadays and every chef has a recipe for it. I only offer mine because I like to use panettone. After Christmas you can buy these cheaply, which I do, and store them until you are ready to use them. The more stale they are the better, and they already contain all the candied fruit and peel you will need. The other name for bread and butter pudding is nursery pudding – total comfort!

SERVES 4

4 eggs

900ml milk

50g sugar

grated rind of 1 lemon

1 panettone, sliced

50g butter

25g currants

pinch of nutmeg

Preheat the oven to 180°C/350°F/gas mark 4.

Beat the eggs into the milk and stir in the sugar and lemon rind. Butter the slices of panettone and cut into pieces. Butter the dish in which you are going to cook the pudding and arrange the panettone slices inside it, scattering currants between the layers. Pour over the egg/milk mixture and leave to stand for at least 1 hour so it all soaks in.

Grate some nutmeg over the top and dot with a little more butter. Bake in the preheated oven for 45 minutes.

Steamed syrup pudding

No book of comfort food would be complete without a steamed treacle sponge pudding. In this age of microwaves it tends to be served disappointingly dry; still, surely nothing can equal the joy of being served this most traditional of dishes, particularly on a cold day, after some invigorating outdoor activity.

SERVES 4

200g self-raising flour

110g butter

110g sugar

pinch of salt

1 large egg, beaten

4–5 tablespoons milk

250g golden syrup (or black treacle)

Rub the flour and butter to a breadcrumb consistency. Add the sugar and salt, then mix to a soft dropping consistency with the egg and the milk.

Grease a 600ml pudding basin and line with the syrup or treacle. Pour in the mixture and cover with greaseproof paper. Place the pudding basin in a saucepan half-filled with boiling water. Cover and steam for 2 hours.

Serve with custard or cream.

Chocolate coconut squares

This is a treat from my childhood. The chocolate and coconut were deeply exotic to a child of the 1950s, and I can remember helping Louise, our cook, to make these, which made them taste even more yummy.

110g butter

2 tablespoons dark chocolate, grated

50g caster sugar

1 egg, beaten

140g desiccated coconut

225g crumbled digestive biscuits

2 teaspoons vanilla essence

FOR THE ICING

110g butter

2 tablespoons double cream

275g icing sugar

Melt the butter, chocolate and sugar over a low heat. Remove from the heat, then stir in the egg, desiccated coconut, crumbled biscuits and vanilla essence. Pour the mixture into a 30 x 22cm Swiss roll tin. Smooth the top and chill in the fridge for 30 minutes.

For the icing, cream the butter, stir in the cream, sift in the icing sugar and beat until smooth. Spread over the chilled base and return to the fridge to chill. Mark into 2.5cm squares. Cut and eat.

Maids of honour

There are many, many recipes for the little tarts that Henry VIII named for his wives' ladies-in-waiting (some of whom he married). I have seen recipes using wet and dry curds, with mashed potato and even clotted cream. I suspect that given Henry's Yorkshire connection they may well have been curd cakes. However, this is a comfort book, not a history book, so I have given you the recipe that I like the best.

MAKES 12

FOR THE PASTRY

225g plain flour

135g butter

2 teaspoons icing sugar

1 egg yolk, beaten with 1 teaspoon cold water

FOR THE FILLING

50g unsalted butter

75g caster sugar

1 heaped teaspoon self-raising flour

2 egg yolks

100g ground almonds

shredded rind of 1 lemon

1 tablespoon thick cream

6 tablespoons quince jelly

Mix all the pastry ingredients together to form a soft dough. Set aside to rest for 30 minutes.

Preheat the oven to 200ºC/400ºF/gas mark 6. Roll out the pastry and use a pastry cutter to cut 12 rounds to fit a 25cm tartlet tin.

To make the filling, cream the butter and sugar together thoroughly then stir in the flour. Beat in the egg yolks, followed by the almonds, lemon rind and then the cream.

Put a little quince jelly in each pie dish then spoon in the filling mixture. Bake the tarts in the preheated oven for 20 minutes, then leave to cool on a rack. Dust with icing sugar before serving.

Boiled fruit cake

This is an Irish recipe and may well have come from my grandmother who lived in a tent! Its name reflects its method of cooking and it is very easy – foolproof, in fact.

It is nice to have a cake about the place, so you can put a slice in your pocket for a hunting, shooting or fishing trip. You can add all sorts of things to a boiled fruit cake; I ate a sensational one made by the 2008 Chairman of the Sandringham WI which contained pineapple. Try this one.

75g golden syrup

125–150ml water

100g caster sugar

100g currants

100g sultanas

100g butter

225g plain flour

½ teaspoon baking powder

1 teaspoon mixed spice

1 teaspoon ground ginger

1 egg, beaten

Boil the syrup, water, sugar, currants, sultanas and butter together in a saucepan, stirring occasionally. Remove from the heat and leave to cool.

Preheat the oven to 180ºC/350ºF/gas mark 4.

Sift the flour, baking powder, mixed spice and ginger together and fold into the cooled, boiled mixture. Mix in the beaten egg, then spoon into a greased 18cm cake tin. Bake in the preheated oven for 1½–2 hours, until a skewer inserted in the middle of the cake comes out clean.

Fig sly cake

I really don't know why these are called 'sly' cakes. The Cumberland and Lancashire versions are made with rum, which dates them back to the 17th century and West Indian trading. Since I stopped drinking I've started making this version of the cakes, using dried figs, which I have resuscitated in boiling water.

FOR THE PASTRY

250g plain flour

100g butter

50g caster sugar

1 egg yolk, beaten with water to make 50ml

pinch of salt

FOR THE FILLING

75g chopped cooked figs

40g chopped walnuts

25g currants

10g raisins

25g caster sugar

Mix the pastry ingredients together to make a stiff dough. Leave to rest in the fridge for 30 minutes.

Preheat the oven to 220ºC/245ºF/gas mark 7. Roll out the pastry into two thin rounds.

To make the filling mix all the ingredients together. Place the mixture on one round, then lay the other on top. Moisten the edges of the pastry and seal well. Put the cake on a greased baking sheet and brush the top with a sugar-and-water glaze. Bake for 20 minutes.

Jam roly-poly

When I was a young barrister, the Croydon Crown Court served disgusting over-boiled cabbage and all things nasty, but amidst all of this was a most perfect jam roly-poly. This is pure comfort food and should be eaten with lashings of custard.

SERVES 4

275g sweet suet pastry

225g jam

grated rind of 1 lemon

FOR THE PASTRY

450g plain flour

225g shredded suet

175g caster sugar

25g baking powder

300ml milk

To make the pastry, mix all the dry ingredients together to form a stiff dough, adding the milk, as required.

Roll out the pastry to a strip 25cm long and 5mm thick. Spread with the jam, leaving a 1cm strip clear all round. Sprinkle with the grated lemon rind. Roll up, sealing the edges well with milk.

Dip a pudding cloth in boiling water, wring it out and sprinkle the inside with flour. Tie the roll in the pudding cloth, leaving room for expansion and tie the ends securely. Boil for 1½ hours and serve with custard.

Parlies

These thin ginger biscuits were served to members of the Scottish parliament before its dissolution 300 years ago. I rather hope that Alex Salmond might restore the tradition!

100g black treacle
100g butter
225g plain flour

2 teaspoons ground ginger
100g soft brown sugar

Preheat the oven to 160ºC/325ºF/gas mark 3.

Melt the treacle and butter over a gentle heat. Fold in the flour and ginger then add the sugar. Mix to a stiff dough and roll out very thinly. Set on greased baking trays, mark into squares and bake in the preheated oven for 35 minutes. Separate the squares whilst still warm. Leave to cool and put in a tin before you eat them all!

Oldbury tarts

This is a Gloucestershire recipe; I like to think the tarts are named after Sir John Oldbury, who was the model for Shakespeare's Falstaff, but I fear this is only my whimsy.
Oldbury tarts are delicious for picnics. You can also make a large version, which you bake for 15 minutes at 220ºC/245ºF/gas mark 7, then reduce the heat to 160ºC/325ºF/gas mark 3 and bake for a further 45 minutes. When it is cooked pour 175g melted apple jelly into the pie and leave to set. Both versions are delicious.

FOR THE HOT-WATER CRUST PASTRY
450g plain flour
100g lard
300ml hot water

FOR THE FILLING
700g gooseberries (topped and tailed)
175g demerara sugar

Preheat the oven to 200ºC/400ºF/gas mark 6.

To make the pastry, sift the flour into a mixing bowl. Melt the lard in a saucepan with the hot water and pour onto the flour. Mix quickly with a wooden spoon. When the mixture has got to a point when you can handle it, knead until the pastry is smooth and free from cracks and all the flour is worked in.

Raise the pastry, whilst still warm, into 6 pie shells, reserving a third of the pastry for the lids.

Fill with the gooseberries and sprinkle over the sugar. Cover with lids and cook in the preheated oven for 30–40 minutes until golden brown.

Eat hot or cold with cream.

Treacle tart

Treacle tart is an easy and much-loved pudding for which, in an emergency, you are always likely to have everything to hand. I usually make mine as an open tart, but you can make a slightly different version, making it into a lidded pie. In Yorkshire they add grated apples, the grated rind and juice of a lemon and dried fruit, but I'm a purist when it comes to this ultimate comfort food.

SERVES 4

200g sweet shortcrust pastry

175g fresh white breadcrumbs

450g golden syrup

Preheat the oven to 220ºC/245ºF/gas mark 7.

Line a small flan tin with the pastry and bake blind for 15 minutes. Simply pour on the syrup and sprinkle on the breadcrumbs. Bake in the preheated oven for 15 minutes, then reduce the heat to 180ºC/350ºF/gas mark 4 and bake for a further 30 minutes.

Chocolate bakewell pudding

This tart is properly called a pudding. The story of the Bakewell political tavener whose kitchen made poured the almond mixture into a jam tart is the most famous example of a sucessful cookery mistake and is probably apocraphal but I shall be banned from Bakewell if I say so. This chocolate version is quite delicious and an

FOR PASTRY

75g unsalted butter

140g plain flour

25g caster sugar

1 egg yolk

2 tablespoons water

FOR THE FILLING

3 tablespoons dark chocolate, grated

150g butter

150g caster sugar

75g self-raising flour

3 eggs, lightly beaten

1 teaspoon vanilla essence

150g ground almonds

grated zest of 1 lemon

3 tablespoons lemon juice

6 heaped tablespoons raspberry jam

icing sugar

Preheat the oven to 220°C/425°F/gas mark 7.

Work the pastry ingredients together to form a dough, and chill in the fridge for 30 minutes. Roll out the pastry and use to line a loose-bottomed flan tin that's 25cm in diameter and 5cm deep. Chill again or bake blind for 10 minutes.

For the filling, place the chocolate in a bowl over a pan of hot water, then remove from the heat when melted. Cream the butter and sugar together. Fold in the flour, adding the eggs, vanilla essence, melted chocolate, ground almonds and the lemon zest. Add lemon juice until the mixture is of a dropping consistency.

Spread the jam over the bottom of the pastry case, then spoon in the chocolate mixture. Bake for 15 minutes at 220°C/425°F/gas mark 7, then reduce the heat to 180°C/350°F/gas mark 4 and bake for a further 15 minutes or until the filling is cooked.

Serve warm or cold with cream.

Index

Conversion chart

Weight (solids)

7g	¼oz
10g	½oz
20g	¾oz
25g	1oz
40g	1½oz
50g	2oz
60g	2½oz
75g	3oz
100g	3½oz
110g	4oz (¼lb)
125g	4½oz
150g	5½oz
175g	6oz
200g	7oz
225g	8oz (½lb)
250g	9oz
275g	10oz
300g	10½oz
310g	11oz
325g	11½oz
350g	12oz (¾lb)
375g	13oz
400g	14oz
425g	15oz
450g	1lb
500g (1/2kg)	18oz
600g	1¼lb
700g	1½lb
750g	1lb 10oz
900g	2lb
1kg	2¼lb
1.1kg	2½lb
1.2kg	2lb 12oz
1.3kg	3lb
1.5kg	3lb 5oz
1.6kg	3½lb
1.8kg	4lb
2kg	4lb 8oz
2.25kg	5lb
2.5kg	5lb 8oz
3kg	6lb 8oz

Volume (liquids)

5ml	1 teaspoon
10ml	1 dessertspoon
15ml	1 tablespoon or ½fl oz
30ml	1fl oz
40ml	1½fl oz
50ml	2fl oz
60ml	2½fl oz
75ml	3fl oz
100ml	3½fl oz
125ml	4fl oz
150ml	5fl oz (¼ pint)
160ml	5½fl oz
175ml	6fl oz
200ml	7fl oz
225ml	8fl oz
250ml (0.25 litre)	9fl oz
300ml	10fl oz (½ pint)
325ml	11fl oz
350ml	12fl oz
370ml	13fl oz
400ml	14fl oz
425ml	15fl oz (¾ pint)
450ml	16fl oz
500ml (0.5 litre)	18fl oz
550ml	19fl oz
600ml	20fl oz (1 pint)
700ml	1¼ pints
850ml	1½ pints
1 litre	1¾ pints
1.2 litres	2 pints
1.5 litres	2½ pints
1.8 litres	3 pints
2 litres	3½ pints

To my agent, Heather Holden-Brown, without who this book would not exist.

To Sophie Allen, for her persistence.

First published in Great Britain in 2008 by Kyle Cathie Limited
122 Arlington Road
London, NW1 7HP
www.kylecathie.com

ISBN: 978 1 85626 713 7

A CIP catalogue record for this title is available from the British Library

10 9 8 7 6 5 4 3 2 1

Text copyright © 2008 by Clarissa Dickson Wright
Photographs copyright © 2008 by Lisa Linder
Design copyright © 2008 by Kyle Cathie Limited

DESIGN: Lawrence Morton
PHOTOGRAPHY: Lisa Linder
PROJECT EDITOR: Sophie Allen
COPY EDITOR: Anne Newman
PROOFREADER: Emily Hatchwell
INDEXER: Alex Corrin
FOOD STYLIST: Lizzie Harris
PROPS: Cynthia Inions
PRODUCTION: Sha Huxtable